BULLEH SHAH
A Selection

GW00645266

BULLEH SHAH
A Selection

Rendered into English Verse by
Taufiq Rafat

Introduction by
Khaled Ahmed

OXFORD
UNIVERSITY PRESS

OXFORD
UNIVERSITY PRESS

Oxford University Press is a department of the University of Oxford.
It furthers the University's objective of excellence in research, scholarship,
and education by publishing worldwide. Oxford is a registered trade mark of
Oxford University Press in the UK and in certain other countries

Published in Pakistan by
Ameena Saiyid, Oxford University Press
No.38, Sector 15, Korangi Industrial Area,
PO Box 8214, Karachi-74900, Pakistan

First Edition published in 1982 by Vanguard Publications Ltd. Lahore

This edition in Oxford Pakistan Paperbacks 2015

ISBN 978-0-19-940288-5

Fourth Impression 2018

Printed on 55gsm Book paper

Printed by Color Plus, Karachi

Acknowledgements
Cover Illustration: Abdul Malik Channa

52.	I'm Just a Sweepress	166
53.	The Load	168
54.	From the First Moment	170
55.	Strange are the Ways of my Love	172
56.	Neither Hindu Nor Muslim	176
57.	Obfuscation	178
58.	The Semi-Literate	180
59.	The Story of Creation	182
60.	Love's Arrival	186
61.	Honesty	190
62.	I'm not Talking of Here	192
63.	Desertion	196
64.	Relatively Speaking	198
65.	Because of You	200
66.	Plea for Protection	202
67.	Saturday	204
68.	Thursday	206
69.	Spring	208
70.	Rain	210
71.	Knots	212

Glossary	214
Index of First Lines	222

INTRODUCTION

Bulleh Shah 1680–1758

The afternoon sun beat down on the concrete courtyard of the mausoleum. It exacted penance from the barefoot votaries for a distant deed of injustice to the poet whose dead body had lain out in the sun in 1758, as the mullahs disputed his right to be buried in a communal graveyard. Today the same cemetery, where orthodoxy had refused him burial ground, is mostly in ruins, encroached upon by a fast-growing town whose hard-pressed denizens defecate on its collapsed graves. The tomb of Bulleh Shah in Qasur and the area around it is today the only place free of collective refuse and the privileged of the city pay handsomely to be bauried in the proximity of the man they had once rejected.

The qawwals constantly sing his rebuking lines: *'Tamba chook-chook mandi javain'*. Their feet burning, the votaries run toward the shade of the graves of the city's rich, taking shelter under stone canopies adorned with mosaic paintings of low taste, of the sort seen on the back of trucks. Bulleh Shah lies serenely inside the dilapidated building of his tomb, its broken stone filigree-work proclaiming his indifference to the well-heeled buried around him. Their gaudy presence lends an edge to the line shouted by a hoarse group of qawwals.

Inside the tomb, the Auqaf Department has allowed mediocre Urdu verse composed by the poetasters of Qasur to festoon the walls in colourful banners. A local grandee has contributed a framed couplet of execrable taste in which his name appears more prominently than the verse he has concocted. Bulleh Shah's own poetry is conspicuously absent in this ambience of bourgeois profanity. Lying under layers of tinsel and flower, the poet communes with the cats that sleep leaning against his grave on the cool floor.

Birth and Education

Abdullah Shah was born in 1680 in Uch Gilanian,[1] the city of
Saints in Bahawalpur, in the family of a pious Syed. His father
moved to a village of Qasur, a district of Lahore division today,
where the six-year-old Abdullah received a strictly orthodox
religious training. No one knows how the boy made his inner
journey from received knowledge to an intensely felt heterodox
devotional religion but hagiographic 'tazkiras' narrate that his
teacher Khawaja Hafiz Ghulam Murtaza Qasuri trained two
rebellious personalities; the other was Waris Shah, the author
of Punjabi's greatest romance in verse, 'Hir'. There is no doubt
that the earliest heterodox tradition he imbibed was that of the
Persian mystic poet Rumi (1207–1273). His most rebellious kafi,
and the most popular, 'Ki janan mein kaun' is almost a literal
translation of a ghazal from Diwan-i-Shams Tabriz.

Shah Enayat

Bulleh Shah's relationship with his murshid Shah Enayat is
also in the tradition of Rumi. Hagiographers tell of a dramatic
encounter between the two in Lahore, one outdoing the other
in a display of miraculous powers. Shah Enayat, whose life
spanned the Mughal rule, from Aurangzeb to Mohammad
Shah, belonged to the Qadiriya School of Muslim mysticism
in India. His scholarship of Arabic and Persian was overlaid
with an acceptance of the mystical traditions of the people of
the subcontinent. This openness to local devotional cults was
ironical since the creed of the Hanbali teacher Sheikh Abdul
Qadir of Baghdad,[2] the founder of the School, was originally
opposed to innovative adjustments of this sort. Tazkiras are
significantly revisionist on this point. They are condemnatory
of Bulleh Shah's revolt against the orthodox creed through
Shah Enayat's disapproval of his disciple's deviationist poetry.
Frequent reference to the alienation of the murshid in the kafis is
interpreted through this revisionist gloss.

The earliest themes in Bulleh Shah's poetry point to a
consciousness of two phenomena: an incorrect sense of divinity

among the people and the possession of a divine secret within himself, which was becoming a kind of pain because it could not be told. The saint Shah Enayat, who practised *baqiqat* (direct knowledge) under the careful camouflage of sophisticated Persian metaphor, was dismayed by the rough vernacular expression of his disciple and advised him to desist from railing against orthodox postures upheld by the political might of the Mughal court. Bulleh Shah did not listen:

> '*Every female from near and far*
> *turned up to brief Bulleh Shah.*
> *Listen, Bulleh, they said, it's a sin*
> *to condemn the Prophet's kin.*
> *Those who acknowledge them, you tell,*
> *Will get the one way ticket to hell.*
> *Does sanctity deserve such scorn?*
>
> *It's God's carelessness where one is born.*
> *When I put the pretty ones in their place*
> *the ugly shoved their noses in my face.*
> *If you seek redemption drop this farce.*
> *My caste? I've none, I'm just a man'.*

The last couplet, not translated, emphasised his allegiance to the *haqiqi* aspects of Shah Enayat, while the rest of the poem obstinately resisted the advice that he should pay homage to the Syed paramountcy in religion. Dr Lajwanti gives an even stronger version: '*To Bulleh people give advice. O Bulleh, go and sit in the mosque. What avails it going to the mosque if the heart has not said the prayer? What matters it being pure outside when from inside the dirt has not gone. Without a perfect teacher, says Bulleh, your prayers are of no avail. Into the fire the prayers! in the mud the fast of Ramzan; over the Kalima black has passed. Says Bulleh Shah, the Lord is met from within me, but the people are searching elsewhere* '.

It is said that Shah Enayat turned him out of his house after this. Aware of the Qadiriya custom of *Sama* and devotional dance, Bulleh Shah took to the *sarangi*, the stringed instrument associated with the wandering dervish, and began to sing and dance. His longing for the true knowledge of God and his intense grief at separation from his teacher was expressed in poems that people found irresistible. The *malamatia* overtones, reminiscent of his great predecessor Shah Husain (1539–1593), lent pathos to his utterances which, out of all familiar tradition, came closest to the current Punjabi spoken idiom. *'Teray Ishq nachaya'* perhaps the most popular of his *Kafis* today, expresses his desolation and helplessness in the face of his unavoidable passion and his alienation from Shah Enayat. Seeing that the heterodoxy of Bulleh Shah had a divine source, his teacher finally took him back. The reunion was dramatic. Shah Enayat, approaching a bedraggled Bulleh Shah asked *'Are you not Bullah?'* and got the answer: *'Not Bullah but Bhulla'. Bhulla* meant *lost.*

His allegiance to Shah Enayat was his only concession to form which also provided him a mooring in the Islamic tradition. In nothing else does he recognise discipline, even the prosodic structure of his poetry does not lend itself to any persistent restraint. He absorbed all that was present in his environment and transcended all categories that scholars now wish to impose upon him. His *kafi* is *a kafi* only in terms of its mystical content; compared to him, his predecessors seem to be too hide-bound in the forms they practised. Baba Farid (1175–1265) wrote in *slokes,* Shah Hussain (1539–1593) tied himself to a raga-oriented metre and Sultan Bahu (1631–1691) accepted the restraint of the *bait.* Although cast in varied metre and rhyme the poems of Bulleh Shah seem to obey only the rules of spontaneous speech of the Punjab. The idiom he employs belongs to the Central Punjab,[3] the area covered by Lahore, Amritsar , Gurdaspur, Gujranwala, Gujrat, and Sialkot, which is why the Punjabi of today is able to understand him and feel the impact of his message more than other great Punjabi poets.

Bulleh Shah's Moods

There is didactic emphasis in his lines when he treats the theme of conventional proprieties, calling the orthodox away from empty ritual to what he perceives as true religion. This is the most quoted part of his poetry. It is characterised by a boldness not seen in any other poet. His *'Ilmon bas kareen o Yar'*, *'Mu ayee baat na rehndi ai'*, *'Ab to jaag'*, *'Ik nuqtai which gall mukdi ai'* *'lshq di navin bahar'*, etc. bring out his most *disrespectful* expressions. At a deeper level, his poetry records the suffering of a lonely man who has seen through the facade of the received faith and cannot feel one with his social surroundings. He perceives his faith as love which strains towards union with God. There is a resultant grief of separation from the Godhead perceived as lover. The yearning for complete knowledge excludes all else and includes it by turns, swinging between states of ascetic withdrawal and pantheism. Poems written in this mood contain the pathos of unrequited love. They are confessional poems, outbursts of an extremely vulnerable sensibility, rising to an emotional pitch where the poet likens his love to a disease he cannot escape. His *'Apnay sang ralaeen'*. *'Uth chalay gawandon yar'*. *'Ik toona'*. *'Patian likhian'*. *'Jind kurikki dey mu ayee'*. *'Jo rang rangia'*. *'Dil lochay mahi yar nu'*. *'Dhilak gayee charkhay di hathee'*, *'Ranjha Ranjha krdi'*, *'Kadi a mil yar piyariya'*, *'Ghariali deyo nikaal'*, etc. reflect this vacillation between hope and despair.

Bulleh Shah's depressive outlook was in no small measure produced by the political situation in the Punjab. Some authors begin their discussion of his poetry with what they consider Bulleh Shah's protest against contemporary political and social injustice, an idiosyncrasy which allows a *progressive* label to be pasted on to him. The truth of the matter is, that Bulleh Shah never directly criticised the rulers, and whatever reference to the contemporary situation occurs in his poetry, is random and oblique. On the other hand he appears to be deeply bruised by the upheavals taking place in the Punjab and was depressed by the sufferings of the common man; indeed, it is certain that the situation contributed greatly to his gloomy world view.

End of Mughal Rule 1707

When the last great Mughal ruler Aurangzeb died in 1707, Bulleh Shah was twenty-seven years old, his poetic consciousness reinforced by a maturity of outlook and experience. After Aurangzeb, the halcyon days that the Punjab had enjoyed quickly came to an end. Already badly defended, the North-Western region of the empire became increasingly subject to foreign invasions and inner centrifugal quarrels. A quick fratricidal reshuffle, in the traditional Mughal style, brought Shah Alam Bahadur Shah to the precarious throne in Delhi. When he died in 1712, his four sons promptly started a war of succession, Jahandar finishing at the top of the heap after killing his three brothers. In 1713, he was deposed and strangled by his nephew Farrukhsayyar. The period of royal gore had begun. Farrukhsayyar was soon deposed, blinded, and executed. the Mughal imperial throne was occupied by pretenders for a time, till in 1719, a lineal heir Muhammad Shah ascended it.

The period of Muhammad Shah coincided with the coming to maturity of Bulleh Shah, and both together coincided with the beginning of the misfortunes of the Punjab. The decay of Mughal administration gave rise to small local tyrannies which lasted into the 19th century and formed the character of the inhabitants of the region. The crisis of character in the Punjabi of today is traceable to this period of duress in the history of his land.[4]

Samad Khan's Battles with Qasur Pathans 1721

Muhammad Shah's governor in Lahore in 1721, Abdul Samad Khan, contended bravely with the marauding Sikhs and kept them at bay; but he had to fight a Pathan rebellion in Qasur which brought great hardship on the people who were repeatedly required to cough up taxes to finance the internecine armies. Husein Khan, the Pathan ruler, won a couple of battles against the Afghan generals sent against him but eventually lost out to fresh reinforcements. In 1737, after Abdul Samad Khan's death, his son Zakaria Khan had to face a more intensified plundering campaign by the Sikhs. The invasion of Nadir Shah in 1738, who spared Lahore but exacted a heavy ransom, further weakened the central rule. Marauding Sikh bands formed themselves into robber baronies and imposed their own system of extortion on the Punjab farmer. Bulleh Shah makes a forlorn reference to this state of affairs in his *'Hun a mil yar piyariya'*. Zakaria Khan's son it was who enacted the general massacre of the Sikhs at Shaheed Ganj in Lahore in 1746, twelve years before Bulleh Shah's death, and perpetuated the resistence begun under Guru Govind Singh. Next year, the Lahore Governor, fearing intrigue against his rule in Delhi, invited the Afghan ruler Ahmad Shah Abdali to India but himself fled to Delhi upon his arrival at the portals of Lahore.

In the highlanders' tradition Abdali was obsessively given to plunder. His treatment of the Punjab weakened the government in Lahore and delivered the various *doabs* into the hands of the Sikh confederacy called the *misls*. Before he died, Bulleh Shah was fated to see a second invasion of the Punjab by Ahmad Shah Abdali in 1748 and then a third in 1752. The redoubtable Lahore governor Mir Mannu fought manfully but unsuccessfully against the invader. Snapping at his heels while he gave battle to Ahmad Shah was Shahnawaz, a claimant of the Lahore throne, which did not bode well for the war and Mannu was at last defeated. As Bulleh Shah lay dying in 1758 at the age of 78, the rape of the Punjab was proceeding apace.

Sufism or Advaita?

The scholarly probing into the origins of Bulleh Shah's mysticism has become a bit of a bore over the years. Dr Lajwanti began this most self-defeating and colourless exercise by categorising the various *phases* in his poetry as Islamic Sufism, *Bhakti Vasnaivism*, and triumphantly discovered the apex of his poetic genius in the achievement of monistic *advaita* in such *kafis* as *'Ranjha Ranjha kardi'*, *Paehli pauri prem di'* and *'Bhavain jan na jan'*. She claimed that in *'Ki janan main kon'* Bulleh Shah finally broke with his Islamic background and merged with the more immanent Hindu philosophy of Advaita, unaware that the *kafis* were literally inspired by Rumi's ghazal *'Cheh Tadbir ai musalmanan'*. Muslim authors, their hackles up, just as assiduously pushed him back into the Islamic fold by pasting on him the exclusive label of Ibn Arabi's *'Wahdat-ul-Wujud'*. But beyond and above this communal humbug, Bulleh Shah seems to incorporate and transcend all the contemporary influences till only a voice remains, the essential and irreducible inflection of the speech of the common man living under the yoke of political and religious tyranny.

Origins of Punjabi

The voice of Bulleh Shah recedes and coalesces with all such voices of the past and his antecedents are coterminous with the linguistic history of the region. British scholars like Grierson and Bailey[5] had categorized Punjabi as a Prakrit off-shoot of Sanskrit—the language of the Aryans—consigning the Dravidian linguistic tradition to the languages of South India, Tamil, Telugu, Kannada, and Malayalam. After a century of acceptance, Punjabi researchers led by Ain-ul-Haq Faridkoti,[6] have begun to claim that Punjabi is a Dravidian language; and Prakrit, instead of being a spinoff from Sanskrit at the mass level, was a Dravidian idiom which in fact transformed Sanskrit and created in it the similarities with Punjabi, which the British scholar mistook as an evidence of the genesis of Punjabi. But the Punjabi scholar is humbled by the fact that he cannot trace literary development in his language parallel to the developments in other Dravidian languages. There is a total blackout of record before Baba Farid (1175–1265), whose vocabulary is quite sophisticated. Between him and Shah Husain (1539–1593), there is another gap of three hundred years during which Punjabi literature might not have existed at all.

The literary tradition in India goes back more than three thousand years, mostly in Sanskrit. Early custodians of the poetic art were priests who held a special caste status among the Aryan tribes. The hymns to various Aryan deities composed by these Brahmanas were compiled with the passage of time into the basic Aryan book called the *Rig Veda*. Other books, the later Vedas, were compiled somewhere around 1300 BC in a Sanskrit which is more or less the purest early version. Three hundred years later, it became mixed with a local Eastern dialect but it continued to be used in this approximate form for another three centuries. A progressive interaction with local dialects began after that till the Sanskrit grammar of Panini fixed the usage in the fourth century AD for all times to come. By receding from popular usage Sanskrit retained its classical form but ceded its status of common idiom to Prakrit which became widespread by the time of Buddha and Mahavira in the seventh century BC.

The Western scholars consider Prakrit an Aryan off-shoot which took on local colour and emerged as a number of Indo-Aryan languages from 500 BC to AD 1000. The earliest written evidence of Prakrit is found in the dramas which figured the speech of the common man in juxtaposition with Sanskrit spoken by the upper-caste characters. The median stage called the Apabrahmsa, when Prakrit was shading off into the modern languages, is exemplified in the fourth act of Kalidasa's play '*Vikramorvasiya*'. Maharashtri and Maghadi Prakrits of this period are known in literary form, but the Gandhari Prakrit in the area now covered by Punjabi is almost without literary trace. By AD 1,000, the Indo-Aryan languages, based on Prakrits, came to assume their modern structure. In the western region, Punjabi, together with Sindhi, has been categorized within this group.

The pre-Aryan languages were of Dravidian origin and they have survived in the present groups called Dravidian and Munda. The first group, spoken in Madras (Tamil), Kerala (Malayalam), Andhra (Telugu), and Karnataka (Kannada) began to practise literary expression with the beginning of the Christian era, while the second group called the Munda, and exemplified by the tribal dialect Brahui, have remained non-literary.

Bhakti Devotionalism

The tradition of *bhakti* in Indian poetry has been condemned by orthodox Pakistani writers as a Hindu inroad into the pure Islamic Sufi tradition. This criticism is more political than scientific. Bhakti was in fact a Dravidian revolt against the Aryan sacerdotalism and philosophy. In substance, it turned away from the polytheism and ritualism of the Aryan Brahamana and reverted to a monotheism celebrated not through ritual but through an intensely individualised devotionalism. In form, it drove Sanskrit and its stiff prosodic regulations out of currency and established an amorphous tradition of composition close to the patterns of localised speech. The earliest *bhakti* poet was a Tamil, Ramanuja (d.1137) followed by Kanarese Madhva (1197–1276) and Telugu Nimbarka in AD thirteenth century. In the west, during this period, Baba Farid (1173–1265) was writing his *slokes* in this same tradition from an Islamic Sufi base. It seemed a reaction of the underprivileged to the domination of caste.

Early Tradition

Maharashtrian Namdev (1270–1350) rejected asceticism and aspired to the knowledge of one God through love in the confessional vein so pronounced in Baba Farid and Bulleh Shah. Tukaram (1598–1650) is the greatest Maharashtrian in the Bhakti tradition, overpowered by love, by the presence and absence of his Lord, and haunted by what he called *'the dark night of the soul'*. In the thirteenth century Bengal, the revolt was led by Chandidas whose poems strongly recall Bulleh Shah.

It is with the development of *khari boli* or latter-day Hindostani, however, that Bulleh Shah's true antecedents begin to assume a distinct complexion. The didactic, reformist, egalitarian, and iconoclastic aspects, in no small measure influenced by Islamic Sufism, emerge clearly in the poetry of Kabir (1440–1518). In diction his poetry is rough, deliberately breaking with the formalistic proprieties, while the message is eclectic, mixing Vedantic monism with Islamic Sufism. The following lines, condemnatory of the externals of formal religion, bring to mind Bulleh Shah's more forceful *'Ki janan mein kon'* and *'Ilmon bas kareen o yar'*.

'There is nothing but water at the holy bathing places, and I know that they are useless, for I have bathed in them.

The images are all lifeless, they cannot speak; I know for I have cried aloud to them.

The puranas and the Koran are mere words; lifting up the curtain, I have seen'.

Tulsidas (1532–1623) took *bhakti* a step forward by suppressing its clear theological adherence to one selected Godhead and its avatars, and has enjoyed a strong influence on devotional and secular poetry, Mira Bai (1503–1573) was also in his non-theological tradition. She reinforced the feminine attributes of the devotee so strong in Bulleh Shah whose intensely felt loneliness is also evident in her poetry.

The Vacana Tradition

Although Bulleh Shah rhymes his verse, the effect is strongly that of colloquial speech because of his non-poetic, exclamatory-emotive usage. In this quality of voice rather than verse he is very close to the *vacana* tradition of Kannada Bhakti poets from AD 1100 to AD 1200.[7] The *vacana* is a form of free verse which relies for its effect on the spontaneous patterns of the mother tongue, an attraction that remains undiminished in the poetry of Bulleh Shah. It has an oral poetic and a rhetoric which introduces inner restraint into free verse. What is today often put down as corruption wrought by the qawwal may be the unfolding of an oral poetic in the *kafis*.

In the didactic-reformist vein, Bulleh Shah's '*Kar kattan val dhyan kurai*' is close to the Kanarese Chowdayya whose free verse runs as follows:

'Winnow, winnow!
Look here, fellows,
Winnow when the wind blows.

Remember, the winds
are not in your hands,

> *Remember, you cannot say*
> *I'll winnow, I'll winnow*
> *tomorrow'.*

Bulleh Shah creates his parallel poem with a more dexterous employment of localised metaphor:

> *'Lass, look to your spinning*
>   *The new cotton crop is in.*
>   *Take it for scouring, and then*
>   *sit down to spin and spin,*
>   *or spinning time will be gone*
> *Lass, look to your spinning'.*

He goes on, in a much more bold and impudent fashion, to emphasise this *mystical opportunism* in *'Kuttay taithon uttay'* and a number of other memorable *kafis*.

The twelfth century Kannada poems are represented by the orally retained works of Basvanna, Dasimayya, Mahadeviyakka, and Allama Prabhu. Two characteristics were distinct in this poety, it broke with the conventional polytheistic religion conveyed through Sanskirt and took one God, Siva, for celebration in a local dialect; and it assumed an iconoclastic tone which subverted the orthodoxy and delivered sharp rebuke to the spiritually complaisant. Both these characteristics are observable in Bulleh Shah. The Kannada poems also contain Bulleh Shah's sense of pain in the role of a *'lover woman'*, the *'Knower of secrets'*. Basvanna's tone is unmistakably that of Bulleh Shah when he exclaims:

> *'Siva, you have no mercy*
> *Siva, you have no heart*
> *Why did you bring me to birth*
>   *Wretch in this world,*
>   *exile from the others?'*

Basvanna's description of his pain in the service of a secret knowledge is graphic, somewhat like Bulleh Shah's *'Jind kurikki deh munh aiee'*:

> *'Don't take on*
> *this thing called Bhakti:*
> *like a saw*
> *it cuts when it goes*
> *and it cuts again*
> *when it comes.*
> *If you risk your hand*
> *with a cobra in a pitcher*
> *will it let you*
> *pass?'*

In another *vacana* he catches the mood of Bulleh Shah's songs when he says:

> *'Feet will dance*
> *eyes will see,*
> *tongue will sing*
> *and not find content.*
> *What else, what else*
> *Shall I do?*
>
> *I worship with my hands,*
> *the heart is not content.*
> *What else shall I do?'*

Mahadeviyakka, a younger contemporary of the Kannada poet Basvanna, embodied in her career as a devotee of the personal god all the tribulations that Bulleh Shah describes through his assumed female identity. Courted by a King and pursued by many others for a conventional marriage, this remarkable 12th century woman brought into vogue the concept of the God as an illicit lover, to which Bulleh Shah also refers when he experiences direct knowledge through *god-as-thief*. Mahadeviyakka's lament about unrequited love and its suffering, the pain of involvement with an unattainable relationship, is also familiar: 'O *Mother, I burnt in a flameless fire*/O *Mother, I suffered a bloodless wound*'. Bulleh Shah's *kafi* '*Meri Bukkal dey wich chor*' echoes in her '*vacana*':

> '*He bartered my heart*
> *looted my flesh*
> *claimed as tribute*
> *my pleasure*
> *took over*
> *all of me*'.

The theme of self-abasement as a confessional approach to divine relationship is deployed most effectively in Bulleh Shah's '*Mein Chuhri an*', which goes like this:

> ' *I am just a sweepress.*
>   *Hair uncombed, barefoot, I receive word*
>   *of his coming. ...*
>   *... Being untouchable none comes near*
>   *me...*
>   *This is my life: cold and sickness and scorn;*
>   *an empty stomach, clothes that are torn,*'

Mahadeviyakka puts it more directly from her status of a woman, but the condition described is remarkably similar. There is a bond of identical experience which becomes striking when her poem is juxtaposed with the *kafi*.

> '*O brothers why do you talk*
>   *to this woman,*
>   *hair loose,*
>   *face withered,*
>   *body shrunk?*

O fathers, why do you bother
*   with this woman?*
*   She has no strength of limb*
*   has lost the world*
*   lost power of will,*
*   turned devotee'*

In another *vacana: ' I love the Handsome One'* she does not only echo some of Bulleh Shah's most favourite themes but also the songs left behind by his predecessor poets, Shah Husain and Baba Farid.

'I love the Handsome One
*   he has no death*
*   decay nor form*
*   no place or side*
*   no end nor birth marks*
I love him O mother... Listen;

I love the Beautiful One
*   with no bond nor fear*
*   no landmarks*
*   for his beauty.*
Take these husbands who die,
*   decay, and feed them*
*   to your kitchen fires'*

By describing the attributes of One God, she is laying bare the impotencies of the gods worshipped in the Hindu tradition. This theme is familiar in Bulleh Shah when he criticises the falsehood of convention in his own environment. In fact his most popular *'kafis'* carry this consistent iconoclastic strain, a quality which distinguishes him from the other poets in the Punjabi tradition. The Kannada poet Basavanna encompasses this theme beautifully in his poem *'How can I feel right'*.

How can I feel right
    about a god who eats up lacquer and melts,
    who wilts when he sees fire?
How can I feel right
    about gods you sell in your need,
    and gods you bury for fear of thieves?

Kannada poets had gone to the local dialect and free verse in revolt against the formalism of Sanskrit and created a complex oral poetic. Bulleh Shah, a man of great erudition as we shall see, composed in sophisticated metrical form, created complex rhyme schemes as no other practitioner of Punjabi verse has done before and since his times. Yet he succeeds in getting across a rough oral effect, as if the poems he composed were a spontaneous everyday expression. He achieves this effect, which takes him into the fold of Kannada oral poets, mainly through the device of first line refrain. Most of his *'kafis'* contain refrains which are meticulously non-poetic and are taken from common conversation. This device immediately rivets the attention of his audience and brings the listener close to the experience of the poet.

Oral poetic

The first-line refrains are, therefore, quite famous independent of the rest of the poems.[8] His famous *kafi 'Ki janan mein koan'* has attained the status of a proverb. Similarly, *'Kuttay taithon uttay'*, *'Uth jaag guraray mar nahin'*, *'Meri bukkal dey wich chor'*, *'Ilmon bas kareen O yar'*, *'Katt kuray'*, *'Bas kar ji bun bas kar ji'*, *'Bhainan mein kat-di kat-di butti'*, *'Ki karda ni'*, etc., appear to have been culled from the conversation normally overheard in the homes of rural Punjab. His technique becomes clear once this pattern has been detected. First he puts down a most nonpoetic utterance, like *'Mullah meinoon marda ee'*, then proceeds to add to it a poem which is an elaborate structure technically, containing deceptively facile but constantly varying line and rhyme.

Bulleh Shah's Frame of Reference

The obverse side of Bulleh Shah, to this studiously cultivated roughness, becomes manifest in the breadth of learned reference in his poems. Like Rumi, who is doubtlessly the biggest influence, his erudition in the Quranic and mystical lore is extraordinary. All of Rumi's favourite references are there: the story of Yusuf and Zuleikha, which holds up the parable of Divine Beauty, comes at the top; Mansoor Hallaj, the mystic-martyr, executed in AD 922; Prophet Moses and Mount Sinai as symbols of direct mystical experience; Christ and the Cross; Bayazid, the famous mystic of Khurasan, hero of mystical stories, who died in AD 874; Junaid, the chief of the Sufis of Baghdad, who died in AD 910; the martyrdom of Husain as vindication of mystical truth, Shams-i-Tabriz, the beloved of Rumi; the parables of Nimrod and the Pharaoh; Solomon and his power of mystical speech, etc.

Bulleh Shah does not mention either Rumi or Baba Farid, classics in whose technical and intellectual traditions he was steeped. Two of his *Kafis* are exact quotations from their work, *'Ke janan mein koan'* and *'Neh Wi doongi'*, but he clearly indicates his preference for the rebellious and deliberately uncouth poetry of Rumi when he makes a scornful reference to Sa'adi's *'Gulistan'* and *'Bostan'*, Persian classics on the study of manners in the Confucian tradition.

The ecstatic example of Rumi and his torrent of extempore verse in three distinct metrical forms was obviously the model for Bulleh Shah. Rumi's knowledge of the Quran is profound which he employs to register metaphorical effect; so is Bulleh Shah's and he follows this example by interspersing his lines with phrases from the Quran. The presence of these phrases both in Rumi and Bulleh Shah is evidence of the fact that the poets, for all their colloquial self-abasement, retained the desire to be considered part of the Islamic Sufi tradition. This partly demolishes the communal gloss so often placed on him by those, like Dr Lajwanti Ramakrishna, who claim him as a *bhakta* in the tradition of Hindu monism. As if conscious of this, Bulleh Shah sings *'Holi Kheiloon gi keh ker bismillah'*; in his most 'Hindu' *Kafi* *'Sayyo ni hun mein sajan payoni'*, he employs the largest number of Arabic phrases from the Quran. The reference to Prophet Muhammad (PBUH), as in Rumi, comes frequently as a shibboleth of the poet's firm identity within the Muslim tradition.

Local Colour

Parallel to the above reference-range comes a whole hierarchy, of local eponyms: the most frequently used metaphor is that of the Punjabi romance *Heer* whose author Waris Shah was a contemporary and is said to have studied religion together with Bulleh Shah from the same teacher. Ranjha neatly symbolises the object of mystical love and Heer is an embodiment of the quest that gives rise to the various conditions and moods of which the tradition of *kafi* is made. The classical mystical utterance of Mansoor Hallaj is expressed in the oneness Heer seeks with Ranjha and often attains a pleasant confusion of identities with him. Ranjha also symbolises the mystery of direct knowledge, the folly of pride into which all mystics are liable to fall, the closely guarded divine secret which can only be hinted at but not expressed. Takht Hazara, the birth place of Ranjha, is a mystical idyll which attains the same status in the eyes of Bulleh Shah as the Prem Nagar of *bhakti* tradition and Multan as the seat of the Suhrawardiya school of mysticism. Choochak, Heer's father and Kheras, the in-laws of the heroine, symbolise the conventional environment within which the quest for the divine must unfold.

Bulleh Shah's Politics

Although he clearly expressed himself as being in the Qadiriya tradition to which his preceptor Shah Inayat belonged, Bulleh Shah cuts across the mystical politics of his times. His reverential reference to Multan as a holy city and to Bahauddin Zakariya, the founder of the Suhrawardiya school is frequent. The Suhrawardiya tradition of patronage is diametrically opposed to that of the Qadiriya who practise asceticism and are given to assimilation of local cults. Bulleh Shah's frequent disavowal, however, of partisanship in the Shia-Sunni dispute points to his disapproval of the Naqshabandiya verdict[9] against the Shia sect. He refers to Husain and Yazid once as being symbolic of the conflict between good and evil but considers it in the monistic sense, thus avoiding a clear-cut identification of the sectarian conflict within the South Asian Muslim community after the eclectic reign of the Mughal Emperor Akbar. His scorn of the Shia-Sunni politics is, however, frequently and most forcefully expressed.

Another poetic influence to which Bulleh Shah makes no direct reference is Kabir, but it becomes most obvious in the *kafis* written in the idiom of Kabir, the Hindustani or *khari boli* which demonstrated a popular mix of Persian and Hindi literary traditions. The Vaishnava vocabulary is used in the manner of an adept. The lover as a thief is taken from the parable of Krishna, who appears now as *'Kahna'* of Mira Bai playing his flute, now disporting himself with numerous *gopis* as the immanent manifestation of a single Godhead. His *kafis 'Yeh dukh kahoon kis kay agay'* and *'Bansi Kahna uchraj bajai'* are in the tradition of Kabir and Mira Bai. Bulleh Shah acknowledges influence of this North Indian off-shoot of *bhakti* by making a direct reference to Tulsidas, parallel to his symbolic employment of local romances of Mirza Sahiban, Sassi Punnoo, and romances of the Arabic cultural background are references to Kurus and Pandus of the *'Mahabharata'* and the Rama-Sita story of the *'Ramayana'* in which Ravana and Hanuman figure as two poles of mystical knowledge.

Qasur as Hell

If Takht Hazara, Multan, and Prem Nagar are idylls, the city of Qasur where he lived is a kind of inferno. Two *dohras* make direct reference to the city after the rise of the Pathans, the chaos of moral and political values in it and the consequent suffering it visited upon the common man. In the *kafis,* the passage of the Mughal central authority is bemoaned and there is a veiled objection expressed against the small-time local potentates who created their own in ternecine principalities in the wake of the empire. His *kafi 'Toon kidheron aya kidher janan'* is a *political kafi*

although the clearest expression of political discontent that he
managed came in the *kafis 'Ultay hor zamanay ayay'*, *'Sano amil
yar piyariya'*. As we have observed earlier, Bulleh Shah cannot
be designated a conscientious objector par excellence against
the political despotism of his times simply because he treated
the subject in passing as an ingredient in a total picture he
wished to present. His lack of deep political involvement can be
gauged only in contrast with a political poem of Sachal Sarmast
(1739–1826), an admiring contemporary.

> I have seen a boat in midstream handled by expert oarsmen.
> These oarsmen consider themselves the rulers of the ocean and
> think nothing of Sindh and India. They are a proud people and
> consider themselves rulers, but they are nothing but plunderers.
> Whenever they get the chance they take the goods of others by
> force. Yet the local people put a lot of trust in them...

It is certain that Bulleh Shah's references to political unrest
and social injustice are related most immediately to the state
of affairs in and around Qasur, the city he has condemned
explicitly in his *'dohras'*. Some scholars connect such references
in the *kafis* to the marauding activities of the Sikhs although the
poet does not name either the gurus or their followers. Indeed
a reference to *'satt'* guru in a *kafi* is in a positive sense; another
explicit mystical allusion becomes the refrain to a *kafi 'Guru jo
chahay so karda ay'*. A line, *'bhorian walley rajay hoay'* is frequently
taken to refer to the Sikhs but it may merely point to the Pathan
rulers of Qasur who came out of their defensive underground
fastnesses to rule the area after the decline of the Mughal rule
from Delhi.

Qadiriya Saints and the Sikhs

There is no doubt, that the Sikhs were an enemy in the satrapy of
Lahore, and in the Pathan fastness of Qasur from 1707 onwards.
It may have been politic for Bulleh Shah not to point to the *'bhakti'*
element in the Sikh movement, as indeed seems to be the case in
his *kafi 'choop ker kay karian guzaray nu'*. By the time the poet had
attained maturity Guru Arjun (1563–1606) had already compiled

the Granth, the holy book of the sect, which was in actual fact a compilation of *'bhakti'* poetry including such classics as Baba Farid, Kabir, Mira, Tulsi, and Surdas. Guru Nanak's *slokes,* forcefully repudiating established religions, sound like Bulleh Shah's own *rebellious kafis: 'Modesty and religion have disappeared because falsehood reigns supreme. The Muslim Mullah and the Hindu Pandit have resigned their duties, the Devil reads the marriage vows. Praises of murder are sung and people swear themselves 'With blood instead of saffron'.* Nanak's lines, written during the chaotic Lodhi period, are non-sectarian because in Nanak's lifetime Sikhism had not yet come into being.

Mughal Opposition

There is evidence that the Qadiriya mystical school of Lahore founded by Mian Mir had begun a close sympathetic link with the Sikhs when they had yet to adopt their anti-Muslim posture. Guru Arjun was a follower of the great Qadiriya mystic and had got him to lay the foundation stone of the Harimandir temple at Amritsar.[10] Shah Enayat of Lahore, the beloved preceptor of Bulleh Shah, was a successor to the Qadiriya *'gaddi'* of Mian Mir and could not have inclined to an overt opposition to the spiritual traditions of the Sikhs. Indeed the relationship existing between the two *bhakti* traditions was carried on by such distinct adherents as Sachal Sarmast in Sindh, avowedly a follower of Bulleh Shah, who continued to send his disciples to Amritsar for homage. On the other hand, Bulleh Shah's intense distaste of the Naqshbandi polemic against the Shia Muslim sect comes through quite clearly in the *kafis.* The Naqshbandiya school was in the ascendant at the court of Mughal Emperor Jahangir and Sheikh Ahmad Sirhindi, Mujaddid Alif Sani (1546–1624) is on record as having condemned Guru Arjun as *'a dangerous heretic who is becoming popular with the Muslims'* in his letter to the Emperor. His dislike of the Qadiriya saint Mian Mir is also said to have prompted him to speak to the king against him. Guru Arjun was tortured to death in Lahore on orders from Delhi. Later, after the Sikhs had acquired a military organisation,

spearheaded by Pathan mercenaries, Aurangzeb had Guru Tegh
Bahadur beheaded in Delhi in 1675 for having befriended Dara
Shikoh during the prince's flight to Lahore.

During Aurangzeb's period, the Qadiriya mystics in Lahore
were on the defensive, careful not to offend an orthodoxy
inclined to take severe punitive measures against heretics. The
memory of their renowned poet-mystic Sarmad (named by
Bulleh Shah in a *kafi*) whom Aurangzeb had ordered executed in
Delhi, was still fresh. The reference in the *kafis* to '*the truth which
cannot be spoken*' and '*the truth which cannot be held back*' could
have been prompted by the repressive atmosphere in Lahore.
It also accounts for Shah Enayat's early rejection of Bulleh Shah
as a follower when the latter began to sing his rebuking lines
against the orthodoxy. In the years to come, when plunder
became routine in the Punjab, Bulleh Shah had no choice of
factions. The Sikh marauders under Banda Bairagi (1670–1716)
were to lay waste the whole of the province excluding Lahore
and Qasur, imposing bone-crushing taxation on the common
peasant for the raising of armies on both sides. The governor of
Lahore, Abdul Samad Khan marched on the stronghold of the
Qasur Pathans and the ensuing battles further impoverished the
countryside. A later governor Zakriya Khan paid heavy tribute
to Nadir Shah as he marched twice on Lahore. So extreme
was the depredation caused by Nadir Shah's looting soldiers
that on his second march he did not take the route via Qasur
as the countryside was denuded of all resources. Aroused by
the plunder of the Sikhs, Zakriya Khan enacted the carnage of
Shahidganj in 1746, putting to the sword three thosand captives
of war. That year Bulleh Shah was sixty-six years old; he was
to die twelve years later, a disenchanted man, witness to three
more Afghan invasions of extreme severity under Ahmad Shah
Abdali.

Much is made of Bulleh Shah's mysticism. As in Rumi, it
tends to limit him as a poet and causes him to repeat himself.
The purely mystical expression has collapsed into a kind of
formula over the centuries and the poet often does not go
beyond a ritual of pointing to the ineffable, of assuming the

posture of a repository of secrets that can only be hinted at. Among Bulleh Shah's 156 extant and authenticated *kafis* most contain reference to mystical knowledge, but they are penetrated with social comment which rescues them; yet, a large number of purely mystical *kafis* also exist and they are monotonous in their unvarying insistence on mysticism. Themes and images get repeated endlessly; sometimes even the refrains are the same as, for instance, in *purdah kis ton raakhi da / kiyon ohlay beh-beh jhaki da* and *Kiyon ohlay beh-beh jhaki da / Eb purdah kiston raakhi da.*

Islamic Sufis absorbed their doctrines from Greek sources and these doctrines predated the Greeks in the Indian philosophy of Advaita. Dr Lajwanti claims that Shah Enayat Qadiri in his book *Dastur-ul-Amal* points to the Hindu origin of the mystical doctrines and their recrudescence in Greek thought centuries later.[11] Dr Radhakrishnan dates the rise of monistic thought in Hinduism around 600 BC just before and after the advent of the Buddha.[12] The mainspring of Hinduism's multi-faceted devotional philosophy are the *Upanishads,* hymnals that began to be written during and after the conclusion of the main Vedic Hymns. *Upanishads* are also called *Vedanta,* 'the end of the Vedas'. The movement of *bhakti,* which was a revolt against later Sanskrit domination, arose from this internal Hindu source, Shankara and Ramanuja being the principal exponents of the *Upanishads.*[13] A kind of neo-Platonism was affected by the Sufis through commentaries which they thought dealt with the ideas of Aristotle. Rumi's world-view was moulded by the doctrines of Plotinus but no one ever got to know his name as the commentators of the Greek philosophers in Alexandria cared little for source references.[14] Amid the hotchpotch of ideas adopted by the Sufis the basic philosophy of Plotinus is detectable: the achievement of perfect union with God; there is absolute unity in existence which cannot be expressed. Rumi's monotone of mystical knowledge is very much in evidence in Bulleh Shah but it is mixed with the monism that we find expressed beautifully in *Bhagwat-Gita* through Lord Krishna,[15] and later improvised upon by such great devotional poets as Shankara and Ramanuja.

Seyyed Hossein Nasr, who believes that all Islamic mysticism is based on the Quran and Hadith, explains the eclecticism of *bhakti* as a case, 'where two great religious traditions lived side by side and a person was touched sometimes by the grace of a spiritual figure from the other tradition'.

Reference to Shah Enayat

The system of *envoi* in Bulleh Shah is also a well-established Persian tradition climaxing in Rumi's *Divan*. Among the Punjabi Sufi poets Baba Farid, Shah Husain, Sultan Bahu, who were his predecessors, it is rarely used. Baba Farid and Sultan Bahu had no personal reference to make to an actual preceptor-beloved while Shah Husain's allusion to Madho Lal is indirect. They had, however, the tradition of self-reference, which was greatly popular, and Bulleh Shah frequently allows it, but not to the extent that his three great predecessors did, raising the device to a proverbial level.[16] In the Indian tradition, too, 'the *envoi* existed only in relation to the *avatar* subject to devotion, as is evident in all *vacana* poets of Kannada. It is only in Rumi, therefore, that we find a true parallel to Bulleh Shah's invocation of Shah Enayat at the end of the *kafi*. His system of *envoi* closely follows that of Rumi who calls upon the preceptor-beloved *Shams-i-Tabriz* in most of his lyrics in the *'Divan'*.

The most common reference to Shah Enayat in Bulleh Shah's *kafis* comes at the end of a whole train of suffering caused by separation. The preceptor himself is the subject of longing as, for instance, in *Ab kiyon sajan chir layo ray*. The *kafi* stands as a poem of longing, its mystical meanings at best inferred, and Shah Enayat figures in the last line of supplication. In another kind of *envoi*, Shah Enayat is made to be the source of mystical secrets as in *Ik nukta yar parhaya hai*. When the poet is plaintive about the inscrutability of Divinity and seems to reach a breaking-point of scepticism, as in *Raho raho oay ishqa mareyaee*, his master comes as a reassurance and a recession to faith. Lastly, the *murshid* is called upon to provide solace to a Bulleh Shah deeply hurt by the socio-political realities of his times. There is no doubt that Bulleh

Shah had a passionate involvement with his spiritual guide and wrote most of his *kafis* as supplications addressed to him.

Dominant Metaphor

Bulleh Shah had Rumi's passionate and spontaneous personality whose main problem was not creativity but an external control over creativity. The roughness of their work displays a forceful and irrepressible expression which cannot be held back. Both needed a mechanism that would give them direction and control but Bulleh Shah seems additionally repressed in terms of the Sufi politics of India in which Shah Enayat is a figure of political restraint: *'Bajh vascelay likhiya na jaey / Shah Enayat bhed bataey'*. In Rumi, the discourse centres on Love, Wine, and Beauty; but the aesthetic of Bulleh Shah is more home-spun. He is not smitten with the Persian fondness for wine as evident in Rumi and climaxed in Hafiz; his love is the forlorn longing of a village-girl for a man whom she has accepted as husband; it is the love of an ugly, rejected woman for a good-looking and indifferent lover, all expressed in mystical allegory. At this point Bulleh Shah breaks with the sensuous legacy of the Persians and joins his predecessors in India. His metaphor surrounds the figure of a virgin who passes through childhood, reaches puberty and declines into age. The basic metaphor is therefore the *charkha*, the spinning-wheel, to which the career of a rural woman was permanently linked. When she attains awareness she is taught to spin and is constantly rebuked when she neglects the spinning-wheel and is lured into games more natural to her age. After puberty, she is constantly reminded that she must spin more than an average output because whatever she spins would become a part of her dowry. Reduce this rural phenomenon in voices and the echoes of Bulleh Shah begin to attain deep effe He had a very discerning ear and translated the whole grid sounds and images of the spinner and the spinning-wheel his poetry. He explores all the possibilities of physical deta the metaphor of the spinning-wheel and gives us a monol

Dhilak gayee charkhay di hathee which is unsurpassed in Indian poetry in its sustained anatomy of a physical object.

Preservation of Works

In terms of written sources, the Punjab and indeed the whole of the Indus basin, has always seemed a wasteland to scholars. The ancient cities of the Indus, though highly developed as civic centres, have left behind no decipherable script while parallel civilisations in the Middle East have copious evidence of the cuneiform. In the North, the Gandhara is no less dumb. Taxila is reputed to have been a great university in antiquity, the Vedas are supposed to have been written here, the great king Ashoka is supposed to have studied here, but very little evidence in writing of this great centre of learning has survived. The valley of Swat, riddled with Buddhist monasteries, was the halting place where Hsuang Tsang, the great Chinese traveller of the AD seventh century, rested and copied some of the basic literature of the Mahayana branch of Buddhism; yet no written records have been unearthed in the thoroughly excavated valley. In Sinkiang, one buried city on the Ancient Silk Route has more wood-shavings written in Kharoshti than the whole of the Gandhara put together.[17]

The twelfth century poet Baba Farid, the first of the Punjabi language extant, would have been without trace had not the Sikh saint Guru Nanak taken his *slokes* from a descendant of the poet two centuries later. Farid is a poet of the Granth and has survived with the sacred book of the Sikh religion.[18] Three hundred years later, the works of the second great Punjabi poet, Shah Husain, would have been similarly lost had not another Sikh scholar, Dr Mohan Singh Diwana collected the *kafis* from the bards and published them in the 1940's. A lack of intellectual tradition among the Muslims of the Punjab accounts for this philistine indifference to the classics. Bulleh Shah was treated no differently.

Yet the world was not passing through a dark age when Bulleh Shah lived and sang in the inferno of Qasur. The year he was born, England was well on its way to a strictly parliamentary rule, the Habeas Corpus Act had been passed and Isaac Newton had led the world by the nose into the modern scientific age. He was nine when the English factory at Calcutta was established and was still a teenager when Swift and Carlyle were writing their works of social criticism.

Bulleh Shah died in 1758. A hundred and thirty years later, there was no written evidence of his poetry. Most of it preserved in the singing of the *qawwals,* and minstrels of the countryside. The first compiler of his works was a Sikh, Munshi Diwan Chand, whose collection was bought by a publisher in Gujranwala in 1886, although the first ever book of the *kafis* published was *Kafian Hazrat Bulleh Shah,* 1882, in Lahore. This latter was a compilation of one Malik Hira, which contained 47 *kafis* but was atrociously copied and had mixed the *kafis* with the work of the earlier poet Shah Husain. The first considerable collection was that of Anwar Ali Rohtaki, *Qanoon-e-Ishq* containing 116 *kafis,* published in 1889. In 1896, Prem Singh Qasuri published 130 *kafis;* then an artisan of Lahore *achiq-saaz,* put together another collection in 1932. In 1933, a lady scholar, Dr Lajwanti Ramakrishna did her doctoral thesis on the Sufi poets of the Punjab, which was published as *Punjabi Sufi Poets.* Critics tend to become mordant about her early assessments of the tradition in general and Bulleh Shah in particular but no one has attempted a critical survey that even comes close to her level of scholarship.[19] She was more than a critic; she was a pioneer on the subject and no latter-day champions of the Punjabi language have attempted even a hundredth part of the work she undertook in the 1930's. The *kafi, 'Bulleh noo samjhavan ayan'* was discovered by her directly from the *qawwals.*

The most authoritative compilation of Bulleh Shah's work was published in 1960 by Dr Faqir Mohammad from the Punjabi Adabi Academy, Lahore. It contains 156 authenticated *kafis* in addition to other poetic forms like *dohras, gandhan, athvara siharfis,* and *baramahas.* Dr Faqir Muhammad's edition is today, the only definitive volume of Bulleh Shah's poetry and luckily preserves a high standard of scholarly treatment and an impeccable *kitabat.* In 1976, Dr Nazeer Ahmad publish his selection *Kalam Bulleh Shah* (Packages Ltd., Lahore) based on the choices made by a group of poets and men of letters. Dr Nazeer contributes a clear-headed view of Bulleh Shah in the Urdu introduction to the book and gives a most useful section of notes on individual *kafis* at the end. The need felt throughout the hundred years of Bulleh Shah's printing, to correct the textual corruption of the *qawwal,* finds its culmination in Dr Nazeer's brave effort to restore prosodic health to the *kafis.* After this the Punjab awaits a proper scholarly assessment of its greatest poet, a tryst that may never take place given the regional antecedents in the realm of letters.

Poetic Forms

Bulleh Shah changed the structure of what is called the *kafi* beyond recognition. The only recognisable rule one can apply to this genre is the rhyme which in effect places the *kafi* beyond the pale of any structural regime. Bulleh Shah uses complex and varying rhyme-schemes and does not accept any prosodic regulation; indeed, it seems he cares little for the poetic rhythm of the line. *Kafi,* therefore, is determined by its mood. Baba Farid's *slokes* are called *kafis,* Shah Husain's compositions are *kafis* par excellence but there is no common factor of definition, apart from the content, which is mystical and devotional. Since the Sufi poetry is composed for the minstrel it was natural for it to be absorbed by the elaborate system of the Indian classical music. *Kafi* is, therefore, commonly referred to as a *raga,* which is technically incorrect.

It is just as well that Bulleh Shah mainly wrote *kafis,* or at least that is the extant evidence. He wrote, in addition, *dohras,* some of which are extremely effective; and *baramah, siharfi,* and *athvara,* all of them unfit for proper poetic expression. More technical exercises and entertainments than spontaneous expression, they tend to debase rather than raise the over-all effect of the poet. *Baramah* is a poem geared to seasons; *athvara* is an account of the seven days of the week; *siharfi,* popular with most Punjabi poets, is an acrostic on the alphabet, beginning each line with reference to the order of the letters. A favourite device with Sultan Bahu, the *siharfi* method of beginning a line has contributed nothing to the intrinsic quality of the Punjabi poetry; it has indeed introduced a needless and tedious mannerism which the editors might do well to rid the old texts.

Bulleh Shah's Critics

Punjabi literature in Pakistan is in a state of neglect. The language has become a purely spoken medium and the Punjabis are no longer able to decipher it in the written form. Literature, therefore, is fast receding into the hazy territory of the folk tradition, lived exclusively orally through the medium of the folk-song. In these circumstances, Bulleh Shah, who is a folk source par excellence, has not found a worthy critic of his works. All the writings on him are either compiler's notes, appended to selections of his *kafis*, or essays written in what is purported to be *get-through* histories of Punjabi literature for the MA courses in Punjabi at Lahore's University of the Punjab. Most of them discuss him under the formula of Sufi writings, and point to his *rebellion*, but abstain from pinpointing the essential ingredient of his appeal for the masses. Najam Husain Syed protests against this tendency to label Bulleh Shah a Sufi poet. He attempts a textualist approach in a brief essay but his work is non-methodical and he gives the impression of a poet taking time out to write prose.[20]

A brief but balanced assessment of Bulleh Shah's mystical background is attempted by Dr Tirlochan Singh in *Laalan di Pand*,[21] but the approach remains introductory and rudimentary. A forced Sufi approach is also tried by Professor Sarfaraz Husain Qazi[22] and Hamidullah Shah Hashmi,[23] but both compilations of Punjabi literature criticism are cramming courses for students and are understandably quite routine-ridden about Bulleh Shah. Surprisingly, even Arif Abdul Mateen remains superficial in his essay and is additionally handicapped by a verbosity he has imbibed from Urdu.[24] Across the border, Sikh scholars have tended to ignore Bulleh Shah in favour of Baba Farid and

Hashim Shah, both integrally related to their religion and politics. In 1979, a book of criticism by Darshan Singh Maini, *Studies in Punjabi Poetry* examines Waris Shah but omits Bulleh Shah.[25] The celebrated East Punjab journal *Punjab: Past and Present* has not featured an article on Bulleh Shah over a period of 20 years.[26]

After C. F. Usborne's pamphlet,[27] the 1938 book of Dr Lajwanti Ramakrishnan, *Punjabi Sufi Poets*, remains the standard assessment of Bulleh Shah, although the frog-chorus of later critics does not tire of referring to her insultingly.[28] Commissioned by Alfred C. Woolner, the great scholar of the language who also worked on its lexicography, the pioneering essay on Bulleh Shah relied on written, oral and manuscript sources and remains the best investigation to date on the Qadiriya background of the poet. Apart from her claim about the progression of Bulleh Shah to an exclusively Hindu monistic inspiration, Dr Ramakrishnan's grasp of the basic characteristics of the poet was sound. It is undoubtedly true that her work has now become dated, but no one since has even attempted to write about Bulleh Shah.

The only living critic of Punjabi literature who is clearly worthy of a definitive assessment of Bulleh Shah is Syed Ali Abbas Jalalpuri whose *Wahdat-ul-Wujud tay Punjabi Shaaeri*[29] touches the subject in passing and in a brief treatment gives evidence of a broad framework comprehension that Bulleh Shah deserves. Jalalpuri has already published an extremely readable book on Waris Shah[30] and has demonstrated his mastery of the history of ideas, East and West, in conjunction with a deep textual and philological grasp. Completely unprejudiced with regard to the derivation of philosophy, his sketch of Punjabi poets in the above-mentioned book comes closest to the kernel of Bulleh Shah's poetic genius. Linking the self-deprecatory tradition of the *malamatia* aspects in Sufi poets with similar trends in world literature and philosophy, he achieves a transcendence of local framework now badly needed for a proper assessment of Bulleh Shah. He has not, however, attempted any comprehensive work on Bulleh Shah.

NOTES

1. Basham A. L. ed., *A Cultural History of India* (Oxford 1975). S. A. A. Rizvi in *India and the Medieval Islamic World* 464: 'During the twelfth and thirteenth centuries many merchants, sufis and scholars came to Multan and Uch through the Kurram, Tochi, and Gomal passes. These areas were heavily studded with flourishing centres of sufism and with trade centre'. The state gazetteer of Bahawalpur, *Extracts from the District and State Gazetteers of the Punjab (Pakistan)* Vol. ll (Research Society of Pakistan 1977), 519, lists Uch as an ancient city once situated on the banks of the Indus in Bahawalpur state, identified by historians as the Alexandria, established by Alexander the Great and the birth-place of the author of *Chachnama,* the great historical classic of Sindh. Uch, also called Uch Sharif, is three cities in one: Uch Gilanian, the quarter settled by the Qadiri saints, Uch Bukharian settled by the Suhrawardis and Uch Mughlan settled by the descendants of the Mughal administrators of the region. The lineal saint who ascends the *gaddi* of the Qadiris' possesses such relics of the founder saint Abdul Qadir Gilani, as beads, scissors and cap. Bulleh Shah is said to be a descendant of the founder and was born in Uch Gilanian. Almost all Qadiri saints and *sufis* in India claimed a physical or spiritual link with Uch Sharif, be their actual position as far away as Bengal or Bihar. The hagiographer of Bulleh Shah has, thus, an immaculate background against which to present him to posterity.

2. Memon, Muhammad Umar, *lbn Taimiya's Struggle against Popular Religion* (Mouton. The Hague. Paris. 1976), 62. 'The oldest of Sufi orders, the Qadiriya, derived its name from the Hanbalite Abdal-Qadir al-Jilani (d. *561–1166)* a native of the district of Jilan south of the Caspian. Al-Jilani studied at Baghdad, where he later took up public preaching in 521–1127. There was nothing in his teachings which may have been against the Shariah; these were pervaded by a spirit of charity and humanitarianism. His message simply stressed piety and disdain of worldliness and ephemeral comforts. It seems, strangely enough, that al-Jilani himself had no intention of founding an order. The order that arose after him, in his name, was largely the work of his sons. By far the most peaceful and moderate, the Qadiriya gradually became the most widespread Sufi order and the image of al-Jilani, in glorifying which his spiritual disciples had strained all the resources of their minds, came to supplant the image of the prophet of Islam'. The Qadiriya are not free of the paradoxes of popular religion. In India they were condemned for their innovations *(bidaat),* but their founder was a follower of lmam Hanbal, the source of inspiration for the stigmatised Wahabbi sect intensely hostile to *bidaat.* At the level of popular religion, the Muslims of South Asia accept *hadith,* the tradition of Prophet Muhammad (PBUH), in toto, but also remain fanatical followers, in name, of Imam Abu Hanifa, the Muslim jurist who relied least on the *hadith* for his judgments. In India, the Qadiriya order were late in coming and represent the most freewheeling of the mystical orders in terms of ritual.

3. Iqbal Salahuddin ed, *Laalan di Pand* (Aziz Book Depot, Lahore: *1973),* Asaf Khan in his article *Punjabi Zaban, Ubdian Bolian tay doojay naam,* 32, deals effectively with the dispute of the dialects in Punjabi. He accepts the Manjhi dialect of the Central Punjab as the standard Punjabi language. He points to the numerous Sindhi dialects and describes how the Hyderabadi dialect became standard when the British in 1853, asked the Hyderabadi scholars to write the textbooks for the whole of Sind. Shehbaz Malik in *Punjabi Lisanyat* (Meri Library: 1977) supports him in this view. Asaf Khan relates the diction of all the great Punjabi poets to Central Punjab, but accepts variations of vocabulary in Shah Husain, Ghulam Farid, etc. He dismisses the claims of various Multani, Pothohari and Peshawari writers about separate Saraiki, Pothohari, and Hindko languages and gives forceful argument in favour of a single language subject to regional lexical and tonal shades.

4. *Viewpoint* weekly (23 July, 1981). Columnist Janus has accurately enumerated the ingredients of this lapse from character in his 'Are you a Punjabi?'. A comparable case is the Czech majority nationality of Czechoslovakia whose members often express themselves self-deprecatingly in relation to character. Janus gives a questionnaire in which 'c' stands for the Punjabi response. (1) Personality growth is always a basic issue. It has physical and mental dimensions and different cultures give different priority to the issue. Would you like to: (a) Develop the mind alone; (b) Develop a balance between body and mind; (c) Exclusively nurture the body in accordance with the famous axiom *Jaanan banao.* (2) If you find yourself in the city of Lahore, you will at some time or other develop an attitude toward it, find it too slow or too historical. If asked to describe your foremost thought about it, will you say: (a) It is a dull city; (b) It is an old cultural centre; (c) Lahore is Lahore. (3) Suppose you are a shopkeeper in Anarkali and are faced with the unavoidable problem of the margin of profit. What will your attitude be from among the three given: (a) Let me build up the business gradually, win permanent custom and become a big businessman in the end: (b) I have to keep up with other and match the prices to the demand level; (c) I have got a saleable item for a month, so let me rake in enough for a house in Gulberg and a Toyota for Puppoo; I don't care if I fold in six months. (4) Suppose you are out on a drive and your ultimate aim is to buy a 'paan' at the Liberty Market. You are driving slowly but someone obviously in a hurry overtakes you. Your reaction would be: (a) The poor man seems to be in some sort of trouble; (b) Couldn't he drive slowly? (c) The jerk! I'll show him by beating him to the next round-about. (5) You have lived in the Punjab all your life, but suddenly you come to know that your ancestor had come here from Central Asia. Your attitude would be: (a) So what, I remain what this land has made me; (b) it is funny how far people can travel; (c) What the hell! I am a Bokhari and superior to all the low stock inhabiting the Punjab. (6) Working in an organization you discover that Pathans, Sindhis and the Baluch tend to flock together. Your tendency would be to: (a) Take a critical view of parochialism; (b) Seek out your own set; (c) Shun your own community, join the others and try sincerely to promote their

interests. (7) In the folktale *Sohni-Mahinwal,* Sohni crosses a big river each night on a pitcher to be together with Mahinwal on the other bank. Upon reading the story you exclaim: (a) Why couldn't the rotter swim across himself and not expose his sweetheart to danger; (b) Great woman; (c) Lucky bounder! A good meal followed by pleasure with a woman who serves a chap well! (8) You have time for leisure and are attracted to cultural activity. You will: (a) Go to a concert of classical music; (b) Go to see a good movie; (c) Visit one of the expensive restaurants on the Gulberg Boulevard and tuck into a hearty meal. (9) In the folktale: *Mirza-Sahiban,* Mirza Khan makes Sahiban elope with him on her wedding night. As they emerge from her bridal chamber at dawn and make their way through the sleeping wedding-party, Mirza puts the back of his hand to his mouth and produces a loud *barrhak.* He challenges the bridegroom and informs him that he is taking his bride. As a result, Mirza and Sahiban are given chase by close to a thousand men on horses. After riding like hell, the two approach a *jand* tree. Mirza dismounts and tells Sahiban that he wants a snooze under the tree. While he sleeps, Sahiban knows that they will be overtaken. She empties Mirza's quiver of arrows so that he does not kill her brothers before going to his own guaranteed death. As a result, Mirza is fatally wounded and Sahiban has to commit suicide. Your reaction to the story is: (a) Stupid ass! Bitched a heroic situation and betrayed a good woman; (b) Both deserved the fate they met; (c) This Sahiban dame turned out to be such a double-crosser. Never trust a woman! (10) All regional languages in Pakistan are taught in schools except Punjabi. All regional languages in Pakistan possess dictionaries except Punjabi. Your reaction to this is: (a) It is shocking, considering the fact that Punjabi is the richest in folklore and has reached a high level of literary expression; (b) I wonder why this has happened; (c) Makes no difference. My children learn Urdu and English as first and second languages. (11) All regional personalities are moulded by a deep love of their idiom. A Sindhi will read Sindhi poetry and can tell you who is the greatest living Sindhi poet: so will the Pathan and the Baluch. Except, of course, the Punjabi. Your thoughts on this are: (a) It is a matter of shame that I do not know who is the greatest living Punjabi poet; (b) I must find out about it; (c) It is useless. First of all I don't know, but even if I knew I wouldn't like to involve myself in controversy. (12) If you are visiting Lahore, you would like to know who was the hero of the city, purely brave personality who stands as the symbol of the city's identity. The Punjabi will not know. Reactions: (a) Come to think of it, I've never given it a thought; (b) Let us try and decide about a personality; (c) Who cares? The *nihari* with lots of strong chillies and high content of oil should be the hero of the city.

5. Grierson, G. A., *Linguistic Survey of India* (Vol. Vlll, Part 1) Calcutta, 1919; and Bailey T. G., *Punjabi Manual and Grammar,* Calcutta, 1925. Both these works remain basic, internationally recognised, sources. Most of the controversy is over the early conclusions drawn by these gigantic works of field research. Punjabi writers disagree with these conclusions but they

neither have international authority nor any sizeable research on the subject to effectively counter them.

6. Faridkoti, Ainul Haq, *Urdu Zaban Ki Qadeem Tareekh* (Arslan Publications, Lahore:1972). Faridkoti's book is a sequel to Hafiz Mehmood Shirani's *Punjab mein Urdu* (Majlis-e-Taraqqi-e-Adab, Lahore) since it discusses Punjabi as a phase in the development of Urdu in the Punjab. He is now considered the leader of critics opposing the British orientalist view that Punjabi is a Sanskrit off-shoot. He is at pains to show that Punjabi is a Dravidian language. The crux of his argument is presented in *Punjabi Zaban diyan Jaran,* an article in the compilation, *Laalan di Pand:* (ed. Iqbal Salahuddin). He claims that contacts with Dravidians before the advent of Aryans transformed Punjabi into a predominantly Dravidian idiom which was later overlaid with Sanskrit vocabulary. He compares lists of basic words and seeks to establish Punjabi's lexical proximity to other established Dravidian languages like Telugu, Kannada, Malayalam and Tamil. A more in-depth study is, however, needed to overthrow the orientalist conclusions; yet, the *Dravidian* view is gaining ground among Punjabi scholars also as a kind of local chauvinistic reaction to the ancient external trespass of the Aryans. For Muslim scholars, the view is attractive because Aryan civilisation was subsumed by Hinduism and now represents its casteridden social system.

7. Ramanujan, A.K., *Speaking of Siva* (Penguin Books: 1973). This extraordinary book of translations in English presents four *Mirasaiva* poets of the Kannada language writing in the AD twelveth century. In Ramanujan's own word: 'Kannada is a Dravidian language spoken today in the South Indian state of Mysore by nearly twenty million people. Of the four major Dravidian languages, Kannada is second only to Tamil in antiquity and literary tradition. There is evidence for at least fifteen centuries of literary work in Kannada. *Vacana*, pronounced *vachana*, is a religious lyric in free verse which literally means sayings, thing said'. It also means 'prose'. The creators of *vacanas* did not think of themselves as poets, for poetry too was something they had revolted against; it represented the court, the temple and the pundit; the traditions they opposed. They practised a kind of Saivism, the cult of the Hindu god Siva but they called it Virasaiva which emphasized their unorthodox use of the deity as an object of devotion.

8. Bulleh Shah is the most frequently quoted poet in Punjabi conversation. One reason for this popularity is his relatively modern vocabulary. But the other, more powerful, reason is that his lines are essentially non-poetic in terms of rhythm. A non-rhythmical exclamatory quality, with a vocative usage of the proper noun 'Bullha', makes for precise assimilation in common speech. In Punjabi, personal names are declined as in Latin and there is a vocative case which creates special effect. It also leads to creative popular innovations. Very often people pretend to quote Bulleh Shah with a vocative of his name, but the lines are their own, not Bulleh Shah's. For instance, *Bullbya, hor wi neenva ho* is a purely popular fabrication and is totally non-poetic. The tradition already existed in relation to Baba Farid and a number of Sikh gurus wrote poetry using: 'Farida' as vocative. 'Bulleh Shah' is derived from

Abdullah Shah which is non-declinable; from Bulleh it becomes Bullah, and Bullhya, representing dative, genitive and vocative cases.

9. Ikram, Sheikh Muhammad, *Raud-e-Kausar* (Idara-e-Saqafat-e-Islamia, Lahore: 1970), 243. The Naqshbandi order was brought to India from Samarkand in Central Asia. In India, its highest exponent was Sheikh Ahmad Majaddid Alif Sani (1564–1624). The order was opposed to the Sufis and nursed a particular antipathy towards the Shia community. Sheikh Ahmad's treatise *Rad-e-Rawafiz* adjudged them liable to death by execution. It was, in fact, the Turani-Irani struggle taking place at the Mughal court. Emperor Jahangir, whose wife had a Shia background, did not take kindly to Sheikh Ahmad, wrote extremely insultingly about him in the *Tuzuk,* and finally put him in prison. Naqshbandi order was opposed to the Qadiriya saints and recommended persecution of the non-Muslim subjects in the levy of a special punitive tax called *jazia.* Ikram's treatment is defensive because of the rise in Sheikh Ahmad's status in the wake of Hindu-Muslim differences in India.

10. Singh, Khushwant, *History of the Sikhs* Vol. I (Princeton: 1963), 56. The founder of the Qadiriya order in Lahore was Mian Mir (d. 1635) who had come from Sehwan Sharif in Sind. Ascetic and shy of courtly favour, he was extremely popular with people of all religions. He nevertheless counted among his disciples Prince Dara Shikoh, whose wife lies buried near his mausoleum. Khushwant Singh quotes sources on how the Naqshbandi chief Sheikh Ahmad reported against his broad- based mission to Jahangir. The King was not particularly well-disposed towards the Sheikh, but was suspicious of Guru Arjun who had made a show of support of the King's rebellious son, Khusrau. When Guru Arjun died, Sheikh Ahmad was jubilant over the death of 'this accursed heathen', as Ikram quotes from a letter of his. Ikram gives details of the Sheikh's campaign against non-Muslims and against the Qadiriya order. He also indicates his high-level contacts with Qalich Beg, the governor of Lahore in 1602. Jahangir, who kept the Sheikh in his camp after granting him release from prison, seems to have heeded his advice against the Qadiris. Sheikh Ahmad also challenged the basis of the order's view of life, Ibn Arabi's philosophy of *Wahdat-ul-Wujud,* and evolved the Naqshbandi concept of *Wahdat-a-Shahud* which effectively opposed the monistic tendencies in Islamic thought, and separated Godhead from the aspirant votary. Sheikh Ahmad's revival of the *sharia* took firm hold in the reign of Aurangzeb and became the yardstick of orthodox faith. The times of Shah Enayat and Bulleh Shah were therefore, hard times for the Qadiriya order.

11. Ramakrishna, Lajwanti, *Punjabi Sufi Poets* (Oxford: 1938), 45. Dr Lajwanti examines in detail Shah Enayat's publication *Dastur-ul-Amal.* The saint believed in the Hindu origin of Islamic mysticism: 'this knowledge', he believed, 'was carried by the Greek soldiers of Alexander the Great of Greece, from where it was borrowed by the mystics of Islam'.

12. Radhakrishnan, *Indian Philosophy*, 138. Radhakrishnan finds it difficult to decide what the *Upanishads* teach, but opines that monism or *advaita* filters through the teaching of Shankara. 'There is no important form of Hindu

thought, heterodox Buddhism included, which is not rooted in the Upanishads'. According to him, the aim of the *Upanishads* is not so much to reach philosophical truth, as to bring peace and freedom to the anxious human spirit.

13. Williams, L.F. Rushbrook, ed., *Great men of India*, (The Times of India publication), 472. Shankara (circa AD 800) was the first exponent of a reasoned philosophy based upon monism or *advaita*. He was essentially a commentator of the *vedas*, including such great classics as the *Mahabharata*, who relied on the message of the *Upanishads* to fashion a heterodox view of life. The essence of his teaching is reflected in the rebellion of *bhakti*. The soul *(atman)* is one with the soul *(brahman)* which is eternal, unchangeable and attributeless. It is the one and only reality. All else is merely the result of illusion *(maya)* born of ignorance. The phenomenal world is illusionary and unreal, like a mirage or a dream. Ramanuja (1017–1137) was a disciple, in spirit, of the great Shankara and was responsible for spreading the gospel of *advaita* outside their Tamil country. He was less inclined to favour the concept of *maya* and considered *bhakti* not blind love but a reasoned devotion to God. Both Shankara and Ramanuja began the rebellion of *bhakti*, but with the passage of time have been reduced to being pillars of orthodox Hinduism through reinterpretation and scholarly argument.

14. Howat and Taylor, ed., *Dictionary of World History*. Plotinus (AD 204–270) philosopher, probably born at Lycopolis in Egypt, who studied at Alexandria and was an important influence on later religious philosophy, both Christian and Islamic. He was the centre of an upper-class philosophical circle at Rome, and in his preaching advocated a withdrawal from the world. He was refused permission to establish Platonopolis on the lines of Plato's republic. Starting usually from a statement by Plato or Aristotle, he sought to direct his pupils to find a transcendental unity behind the infinitely varied manifestations of the sensible world. His writings were edited by his pupil, Porphyry, into nine treatises called *Enneads*.

15. For instance, these lines which demonstrate the mystic's indifference to the idea of sin and virtue: *The Lord is everywhere / and always perfect what does He care / for man's sin or / the righteousness of man?*

16. Ahmad, Nazir, *Kalam Shah Husain* (Packages Ltd. Lahore: 1979). Dr Nazir in his introduction points out that self-reference in Shah Husain was frequently an interpolation of the *qawwals*, which upset the prosodic balance of the poem. He also notes that Shah Husain makes no reference to his beloved Madho Lal in his *kafis*. On the other hand, Bulleh Shah's invocation of Shah Enayat is constant. His self-reference in *Bullhya ki janan mein kaon* is proverbial in usage.

17. Stein, Sir Aurel, *On Ancient Central Asian Tracks* (Macmillan: 1933). Stein gathered thousands of wood-shavings written in Kharoshti, the Gandharan script, on the Southern arm of the Silk Route. Most of this material is in the British Museum.

18. Khan, Muhammad Asaf, *Akhiya Baba Farid nay* (Pakistan Punjabi Adabi Board, Lahore: 1978). Asaf Khan has put together in this book the latest

research on the provenance of the poetry of Baba Farid (1173–1265). Guru Nanak (1469–1538) collected the great first poet's work from his heirs and wrote it down in his notebooks, which also anthologised fifteen other sufi and *bhakti* poets of India. Guru Arjun (l553–1606) put together the first copy of the Holy Granth out of these notebooks, and thus secured Baba Farid from obscurity. Today, he is the most important poet of the Granth, with more *slokes* than any other selected poet.

19. The bone of contention in Dr Lajwanti Ramakrishna is her assertion on page 54 of the book *Punjabi Sufi Poets:* 'The third and last phase of Bullha's mystic life was unique. Here he resembles no sufi or *vaisnava* of the Punjab or the rest of India. During this time he is a firm believer in *advaita* and sees that all-pervading spirit, God, in all and independently of all religions. Like a true *vedantist,* he does not only see Him in friends, and co-believers, but in heathens and opponents, too'. Discussing Bulleh Shah's famous poem *Bullhia ki janan mein kaon,* she states again: 'We have stated that the pantheism of Bulleh Shah was Hindu in its entirety, and therefore, differed a good deal from the pantheism of the Sufis. His *advaita,* which was Indian in its essence, had so overpowered him, nay had transformed him in such a way that any sort of conversion was beyond his understanding'. At this juncture it would be in order to present the lyric of Rumi on which Bulleh Shah had based his *kafi.* The English translations of the two texts come from Dr Lajwanti Ramakrishnan's book and R. A. Nicholson's rendition in *Divan-i-Shams-i-Tabriz:*

Bulleh Shah

'Bullha, what do I know who I am? Neither am I Muslim in the mosque nor am I in the ways of paganism, nor among the pure or sinful, nor am I Moses or the Pharaoh; Bullha, what do I know who I am? Neither in the books of doctors I, nor indulged I in cannabis and wine, nor in the winehouse in the company of bad people, neither awake nor asleep. Bullha, what do I know who I am? Neither in happiness nor in sorrow, nor in sin or purity, nor of water, nor of earth, nor in fire, nor in air. Bullha, what do I know who I am? I am not of Arabia, nor of Lahore, nor an Indian nor of the city Nagaur, neither a Hindu, nor a Muslim of Peshawar, nor do I live in Nadaun. Bullha, what do I know who I am? Neither have I found the secret of religion, nor of Adam and Eve am I born, neither have I taken a name, my life is neither settled nor unsettled. Bullha, what do I know who I am? Myself I know as the first and the last, none else as second do I recognize, none else is wiser than I. Bullah, who is the true master?'

Rumi

What is to be done, O Muslims? For I do not recognize myself. I am neither Christian nor Jew nor Parsi nor Muslim. I am not of the East nor of the West nor of the land nor of the sea. I am not of Nature's mint, nor of water, nor of air, nor of fire. I am not of the Empyrean, nor of the dust, nor of existence, nor of entity. I am not of India, nor of China, nor of Bulgaria, nor Saqsin. I am not of the Kingdom of Araqain, nor of the country of Khorasan, I am not of this world, nor of the next, nor of Paradise, nor of Hell. I am not of Adam, nor of Eve, nor of Eden and Rizwan. My place is the Placeless, my trace is the Traceless. It is neither body nor soul, for I belong to the soul of the beloved. I have put duality away, I have seen that the two worlds are one. One I seek, one I know, one I call. He is the first. He is the last. He is the outward, He is the inward. I am intoxicated with love's cup, the two worlds have passed out of my ken. I have no business save carouse and revelry. If once in my life I spent a moment without thee, from that time and that hour I repent of my life. If once in this world I win a moment with thee, I will trample on both the worlds, I will dance in triumph for ever. O Shams-i-Tabriz, I am so drunken in this world, that except of drunkenness and revelry I have no tale to tell'.

20. Syed, Najm Husain, *'Recurrent Patterns in Punjabi Poetry* (Majlis Shah Husain, Lahore).

21. Dr Tirlochan Singh in his article *Bulleh Shah da Tassavuf,* concentrates on the Islamic derivation of Bulleh Shah's mysticism in a conscious antithesis to Dr Ramakrishna's opinion.

22. Qazi, Prof. Sarfaraz Hussain, *Tassawuf tay Punjabi day Shaair* (Aziz Book Depot, Lahore: 1973).

23. Hashmi, Hamidullah Shah, *Punjabi Adab di Mukhtasir Tareekh* (Taj Book Depot, Lahore).

24. Abdul Mateen, Arif, *Parakh Parchol* (Jadeed Nashireen, Lahore: 1979).

25. Maini, Darshan Singh, *Studies in Punjabi Poetry* (Vikas Publishing Co., Delhi: 1979).

26. Based on an inquiry at libraries. The author has a file of the journal from 1965 to 1975 which does not contain a single article on Bulleh Shah.

27. Usborne, C. F., *Sain Bulleh Shah* (Punjab University, Lahore: 1905).

28. Ahmed, Nazir, *Kalam Bulleh Shah* (Packages Ltd., Lahore, 1977) Dr Nazir, otherwise of moderate opinion, is unfortunately guilty of the most unscholarly comment on Dr Lajwanti Ramakrishnan when he says: 'This home-broken dame must be serving up *pilao* of peas, *tikkas* of cheese and balls of *saag*, but knows little about poetry'. Dr Nazir tends to be idiosyncratic, and therefore, unreliable at times. For instance in his *kafi Muh ai baat na rahindi hai,* when Bulleh Shah says, 'If I state an untruth something remains (is saved); by telling the truth the fire spreads', Dr Nazir accuses him of positing an immoral proposition, showing no discernment of the device of transference of poetic persona. If this is naive on the part of the scholar, his dismissal, as a mystical commonplace, of the metaphor of the spinning-wheel, central to Bulleh Shah's poetry, is tantamount to tossing the baby away with the bath-water.

29. Jalalpuri, Ali Abbas, *Wahdat-ul-Wajud tay Punjabi Shaaeri* (Pakistan Punjabi Adabi Board, Lahore: 1977).

30. Ibid. *Muqamat-e-Waris Shah* (Aina Adab, Lahore: 1972).

Bulleh Shah
A Selection

A for Allah

A for Allah who has my heart,
I have no knowledge of B,
nor do I know what it means,
while A savours sweet to me.
I can't tell between O and Q,
it makes me dither and delve;
Bulleh, look after the first,
the rest will take care of itself.

لَا اللہ دِل رَتّا میرا

اؔ اللہ دِل رَتّا میرا
مَینُوں بِ دِی خبر نہ کائی
بِ پڑھیاں کُجھ سَمجھ نہ آوے
اؔ دی لذّت آئی
عؔ تے غؔ دا فرق نہ جاناں
ایہ گل اؔ سُجھائی
بُجھیا! قول اؔ دے پُورے
جیہڑے دل دی کرن صفائی

The Difference

O and Q are much alike, except for a squiggle;
to think one tiny stroke has made the whole world wriggle.

حَبیسی صُورت عِ دی

حَبیسی صُورت عِ دی، وَیسی صُورت غ
اِک نقطے دا فرق ہَے: بُھلی پھرے گوئیں

Wayfarer, Arise

The last stars have been scrubbed from the skies.
Wayfarer, arise!
> The camp is astir, you are too slow,
> your companions are ready to go.
> Are you deaf to the clangour and cries?
Wayfarer, arise!
> Up, up, from too much fuss retrain,
> for you will not come this way again;
> the rest are saddled up, unwise.
Wayfarer, arise!
> You check each article you own
> when none will help. So much to be done
> and you laze in bed with tight-shut eyes.
Wayfarer, arise!
> Bulleh, you need to re-dedicate
> yourself to action. This inert state,
> like a neglected field, all growth denies.
Wayfarer, arise!

اَب تو جاگ!

اَب تو جاگ مُسافر پیارے
رین گئی، لٹکے سب تارے
آواؤن سرائیں ڈیرے
ساتھ تیار مسافر تیرے
اَجے نہ سُنیوں کُوچ نقارے
اَب تو جاگ مُسافر پیارے

گُرلے اَج گرنی دا ویرا
مُڑ نہ ہوسی آون تیرا
ساتھی چلّو چل پُکارے
اَب تو جاگ مُسافر پیارے

موتی، چُونی، پارس پاسے
پاس سمندر، مرو پیاسے
کھول اَکھیں، اُٹھ بوہ بیکارے
اَب تو جاگ مُسافر پیارے

بلّھا! شوہ دے پیریں پڑیے
غفلت چھوڑ کُجھ چیلہ کریے
مرگ جتن بِن کھیت اُجاڑے
اَب تو جاگ مُسافر پیارے

I Swallowed the Hook

I swallowed the hook, and myself pull the line.

Draw your face to mine.

Uproar in Mecca when a voice came from the sky,
not you, Bulleh, but someone else will die.

Draw your face to mine.

آپے پائِیاں کُنڈیاں

آپے پائِیاں کُنڈِیاں تے آپے کِھچنائِیں ڈور

ساڈے وَل ٹکھُڑا موڑ

عرش کُرسی تے بانگاں مِلِیاں، مَچّے پے گیا شور

بُلّھے شاہ! اَساں مَرنا نابیں، مَرجاوے کوئی ہور

ساڈے وَل ٹکھُڑا موڑ

The Trap

On the ripening corn, the birds descended.
Some were netted, some the falcons ended;
some turned back, some were turned on spits.
Who can escape what the Lord intended?

آئی رُت شگوفیاں والی

آئی رُت شگوفیاں والی، حپڑیاں جگن آئیاں
اِکتاں نُوں حُبریاں پھَر کھاہدا، اِکتاں پھائیاں لائیاں
اِکتاں آسِس مُرن دی آہے، اِک سیخ کباب حپڑھائیاں
بلّھے شاہ! کِہ وَسّ اُہاں جو مَار تقدیر پھَسائیاں

Where is Your Home?

Where is your home?
Whence did you come?
Where do you go?

The place you pride in
will go for a song;
kill, rob the poor,
think yourself strong;
your four days reign
will end before long;
you will soon be put
where you belong.

The Boatman's ferry is full
each time it crosses.
Bulleh, you old sinner,
reckon your losses.

Where is your home?
Whence did you come?
Where do you go?

اپݨا دَسّ ٹِکاݨا

اپݨا دَسّ ٹِکاݨا؛ کِدھروں آیا، کِدّھر جاݨا؟

جِس ٹھائے دَا مَاݨ کَریں توں
اوہنے تیرے نال نہ جاݨا
ظُلم کَریں تے لوک ستاویں
گَسب پھڑیو لُٹ کھاݨا
کرَئے چاوَڑ چپار دیہاڑے
اوڑک توں اُٹھ جاݨا
شہرِ خموشاں دے چل ویّے
جِتّھے مُلک سماݨا
بھر بھر پور لنگھاوے، ڈاہڈا
مَلک المَوت مہاݨا
ایہناں سبھناں تھیں ہَے بُلّھا
او گنہار پُراݨا
اپݨا دَسّ ٹِکاݨا؛ کِدھروں آیا، کِدّھر جاݨا؟

A Safe Place

So that none will run before or behind
let us go to a place where all are blind.

چل بُلّھا! چل اوتھے چلیے

چل بُلّھا! چل اوتھے چلیے، جتھے سارے اَنّھے
نہ کوئی ساڈی ذات پچھانے، نہ کوئی سانوں منّے

Embrace Me, Love

Embrace me, love, and hold me next your heart.
What sinister jungles stand in my way,
what snakes, what beasts of prey,
and on the other side what spirits start.
Reach out your hand to me so fear may cease,
one glimpse of you and I shall be at peace.

Embrace me, love, and hold me next your heart.

اپنے سنگ رلائیں

اپنے سنگ رلائیں پیارے! اپنے سنگ رلائیں
راہ پُواں تے دھاڑے بیلے؛ جنگل، رکھّ، بلائیں
بگھن چِتّے، چِت مِحّے، بگھنے روکن راہیں
تیرے پار جگا دھر حپڑھیا، کنڈھے لکھّ بلائیں
ہَول دِلے توں تھر تھر کنبدا، بیڑا پار لنگھائیں
بلّھے شاہ نُوں شَوہ دا مکھڑا گھونگھٹ کھول دِکھائیں

اپنے سنگ رلائیں پیارے! اپنے سنگ رلائیں

Left Alone

Friends are all falling like hair,
God, what shall I do?

> Nothing can induce them to stay;
> rather, they propagate despair.

>> God, what shall I do?

On all sides news of departures,
and goodbyes echo in the air.

>> God, what shall I do?

Their memories tear me apart;
I see them everywhere.

>> God, what shall I do?

Bulleh, your fondness is at fault;
they are neither here, nor there.

>> God, what shall I do?

اُٹھ چلے گوانڈھوں یار

اُٹھ چلے گوانڈھوں یار

رَبّا ہُن کِہہ کریے!

اُٹھ چلّے، ہُن رہندے ناہیں

ہویا ساتھ تیّار

رَبّا ہُن کِہہ کریے!

چارو طرف چلن دے چُرچے

ہر سُو پَئی پُکار

رَبّا ہُن کِہہ کریے!

ڈھانڈ کلیجے بل بل اُٹھدی

بِن دیکھے دیدار

رَبّا ہُن کِہہ کریے!

بُلھا! شَوہ پیارے باجھوں

رہے اُرار نہ پار

رَبّا ہُن کِہہ کریے!

Spell

I will use a spell
to get my lost love back.
    And breathe this spell on the air,
    the sun will make it warm.
    Black are my eyes and eyebrows,
    they will brew up a storm.
    I have an ocean within me
    whose tides none can becalm.
    Although I am a virgin
    there's a babe on my arm.

    Like the lightning I will flash
    and thunder like the cloud.
    I crackle in love's flames,
    the moon will weave me a shroud.

    I shall roam Iike a gypsy
    and sing my plaint aloud,
    till the sap of my passion
    runs madly through each clod.

اِک ٹُوتا

اِک ٹُوتا اَچنبا گاواں گی
مَیں رُٹھا یار مناواں گی
اِسے ٹُوتا مَیں پڑھ پڑھ پُھوکاں
سُورج اَگن جلاواں گی
اَکّھیں کاجل، کالے بادل
بھواں سے آندھی لیاواں گی
ست سمندر دِل دے اَندر
دِل سے لہر اُٹھاواں گی
نہ مَیں بیاہی نہ مَیں کواری
بیٹا گود کھڈاواں گی
بجلی ہو کر چمک ڈراواں
بادل ہو گرجاواں گی
عِشق انگیٹھی، ہر مل تارے
چاند سے کفن بناواں گی
لا مکان کی پڑی اُوپر
بہ کر ناد بجاواں گی
لائے سواں مَیں شوہ گل اپنے
تَد مَیں نار کہاواں گی

Heritage

What parents sowed, the children reap.
Who's the benefactor? Who the thief?
When the corn came in, the knives came out;
brother fought brother for every sheaf.
One sinned, another bears the grief.
What parents sowed, the children reap.

اَتّاں بابے دِی بھلیائی!

اَتّاں بابے دی بھلیائی ، اوہ ہُن کمّ اساڈے آئی

اَتّاں بابا چور دُھراں دے، پُتر دِی وَڈیائی

دانے اُتّوں گُت بگتی، گھر گھر پَئی لڑائی

اَساں قضیّے تاہیں جاّلے کنک اُنھاں ٹُکائی

کھائے خیراتے پھاڑے جُّما، اُلٹی دستک لائی

اَتّاں بابے دی بھلیائی، اوہ ہُن کمّ اساڈے آئی

One is Enough

One is enough. Break the counting-frames,
forget hell's terrors and its flames,
purify your dreams and desires,
belief and unbelief are just names.

> Truth stands in the hall.
> One point settles it all.

In prayer why abrade your forehead?
Away with it, tear down the facade
of morality. Causing people pain
is the only sin you should dread.

> The writing is on the wall.
> One point settles it all.

To the same jungle the hawks repair
and seed by seed they scrounge there;
in this their energy is spent,
and they are left gasping for air.

اِک نقطے وِچ گل مُکدی اے

پھِڑ نقطہ، چھوڑ حساباں نُوں
چھڈ دوزخ، گور عذاباں نُوں
کر بند کفر دیاں باباں نُوں
کر صاف دِلاں دیاں حِناباں نُوں
گل ایسے گھر وِچ ڈُھکدی اے
اِک نقطے وِچ گل مُکدی اے

ایویں مَتھا زمیں گھسائیدا
پا لمّا محراب دِکھائیدا
پڑھ کلمہ لوک ہسائیدا
دِل اندر سمجھ نہ لائیدا
گُدی سچّی بات وی لُکدی اے
اِک نقطے وِچ گل مُکدی اے

اِک جنگل، بحریں جاندے نیں
اِک داتے روز دا کھاندے نیں
بے سمجھ وجُود تھکاندے نیں
گھر آون ہو کے ماندے نیں

Prayer is body's gall.
One point settles it all.

From a pilgrimage some have returned,
but any merit they may have earned,
despite humility in dress,
in percentage and shady deals is burned.

Truth stands too tall.
One point settles it all.

چلیاں اندر چند شکدی اے

اِک نُقطے وِچ گل مُکدی اے

کئی حاجی بن بن آئے جی

گل نیلے جامے پائے جی

حج وِچّ، ٹکے لے کھائے جی

پر اسے گل کیہنوں بھائے جی

کِتّے سچّی گل وِی رُکدی اے

اِک نُقطے وِچ گل مُکدی اے

A Topsy-Turvy World

In a topsy-turvy world I saw the truth unroll

Crows peck at scarecrows, pigeons fell the hawk,
and asses have assumed the horse's role.

Nor aunt nor uncle now receives respect;
children shun the path where parents stroll.

The old on bare boards sit while newness struts,
liars have mansions, truth has the begging-bowl.

It was so ordained, Bulleh, accept the fact,
on carpets graced by lords the lackeys loll.

In a topsy-turvy world I saw the truth unroll.

اُلٹے ہور زمانے آئے

اُلٹے ہور زمانے آئے، تاں مَیں بھیت سَجّن دے پائے

کاں لگڑاں نُوں مارن لگّے، چڑیاں جُرّے ڈھائے
گھوڑے چُگن اُروڑیاں تے گدّوں خوید پوائے

آپتیاں وِچ اُلفت ناہیں، کیا چپاچے، کیا تائے
پیُوپُتراں اتفاق نہ کائی، دھیّاں نال نہ مائے

سچّیاں نُوں پَے ملدے دھکّے، جھوٹھے کول بہائے
اگلے ہو کنگالے بیٹھے، پچھلیاں فرش وچھائے

بھوریاں والے راجے کیتے، راجیاں بھیک منگائے
اُلّھیا! حکم حضوروں آیا، تس نُوں کون ہٹائے

اُلٹے ہور زمانے آئے، تاں مَیں بھیت سَجّن دے پائے

Not for a Moment

I welcome those who come, bless those who depart,
but not for a moment can I bear to part
from my love. I dream of love, and wake to love,
or scare the crows from my embattled heart.

ایک حرف سی حرفی

۱- آندیاں توں مَیں صدقڑے ہاں، جویں جانداں توں سروارنی ہاں
مُٹھی پریت انوکھڑی لگ رہی گھڑی پل سنے یار وِسارنی ہاں
کیہے ہڈ تکا ڈرے پے مَینوں اونسیاں پاوندی، کانگ اُڈارنی ہاں
بُلّھا! شوہ تے کملی مَیں ہوئی، سُتّی جاگدی یار پُکارنی ہاں

Does Anyone Know?

Who am I? Does anyone know?

In a mosque no worshipper,
nor a temple-frequenter,
I'm not pure, nor impure,
nor Moses, nor Pharaoh.

Does anyone know?

What is good, what badness?
What is mirth, what sadness?
I'm not earth, water, fire,
nor the winds that blow.

Does anyone know?

بُلھا! کِیہ جَاناں مَیں کَون

بُلھا! کِیہ جَاناں مَیں کَون؟

نہ مَیں مومن وِچ مسِیتاں

نہ مَیں وِچ کُفر دِی رِیت آں

نہ مَیں پاکاں وِچ پلِیت آں

نہ مَیں موسیٰؑ، نہ فِرعون

بُلھا! کِیہ جَاناں مَیں کَون؟

نہ مَیں وِچ پلِیتی پاکی

نہ وِچ شادی، نہ غمناکی

نہ مَیں آبی، نہ مَیں خاکی

نہ مَیں آتش، نہ مَیں پَون

بُلھا! کِیہ جَاناں مَیں کَون؟

I refuse to believe.
Who was Adam? Who Eve?
What does my name mean?
I neither stay, nor go.

Does anyone know?

The universe tells
there is You and none else.
But who stands there
in the wall's shadow?

Does anyone know?

نہ مَیں بھیت مذھب دا پایا
نہ مَیں آدم حوّا جایا
نہ کُجھ اپنا نام دھرایا
نہ وِچ بَیٹھݨ، نہ وِچ بھَوݨ
بُلھا! کِیہ جاناں مَیں کَوݨ؟

اوّل آخِر آپے نوں جاناں
نہ کوئی دُوجا ہور پچھاناں
مَیتھوں وَدھ نہ کوئی سِیاناں
بُلھا! اوہ کھڑا ہَے کَوݨ؟
بُلھا! کِیہ جاناں مَیں کَوݨ؟

Briefing Bulleh

Every female from near and afar
turned up to brief Bulleh Shah.
Listen Bulleh, they said, it's a sin
to condemn the prophet's kin.
Those who acknowledge them, you tell,
will get the one-way ticket to hell.
Does sanctity deserve such scorn?

It's God's carelessness where one is born.
When I put the pretty one in their place
the ugly shoved their noses in my face.
If you seek redemption drop this farce.
My caste? I've none. I'm just a man.

بُلّھے نوں سمجھاون آئیاں

بُلّھے نوں سمجھاون آئیاں بھیناں تے بھرجائیاں

''مَن لے بُلّھیا ساڈا کہنا، چھڈ دے پلّا رائیاں
آلِ نبیؐ اولادِ علیؓ نوں توں کیوں لیکاں لائیاں؟''

''جیہڑا سانوں سیّد سدّے دوزخ مِلن سزائیاں
جو کوئی سانوں رائیں آکھے بھشتی پینگاں پائیاں''

رائیں، سائیں سبھنی تھائیں، رَبّ دیاں بے پروائیاں
سوہنیاں پرے ہٹائیاں تے کوجھیاں لَے گل لائیاں

بے توں لوڑیں باغ بہاراں، چپ کر ہو جباّرائیاں
بُلّھے شاہ دی ذات کیہ پُچھنیں؟ شاکر ہو رضائیاں

Wanderer, Ho

Wanderer, ho!
Bring back a word of love, or so,

       wanderer, ho!

Tell him, do not spare the details,
how I am bent double with woe,

       wanderer, ho!

Let not modesty restrain you from
describing how nakedly I go,

       wanderer, ho!

Don't be impatient, take your time
in giving my news; with gestures show,

       wanderer, ho!

Listen carefully to what he says;
then hurry back and let me know,

       wanderer, ho!

پاندھیا ہو!

جھب سُکھ دا سنیوہڑا لیاویں وے
پاندھیا ہو!

مَیں دُبڑی مَیں کُبڑی ہوئیاں،
مـرے دُکھڑے سب بتلاویں وے
پاندھیا ہو!

,,گھلّی لِٹ گل، ہَتّھ پراندا‘‘
اسے کہندیاں نہ شرماویں وے
پاندھیا ہو!

یاراں لِکھ کے کتابت بھیجی
کِسے گوشے سب سمجھاویں وے
پاندھیا ہو!

بُلّھا! شَوہ دِیاں مُٹّن مُہاراں
اے پیتاں توُں جھب دھاویں وے
پاندھیا ہو!

Accursed

He has not come. In the evening I sit
and write letters, The darkness scares me.
I ask each passing magus, why is it
everything I do turns out badly?

Astrologer, be kind, tell the truth
for once. Am I cursed? Was I born ill-fated?
If I could run away, I would, my youth
to beggary give, but with chains I'm weighted.

And even sleep has migrated, that he
may not enter my dreams. His absence sears
my heart. Someone has cast a spell on me
so that my eyes cannot even shed tears.

What was it I gained by love? Tantrum
after tantrum, and nothing but pain.
Yet all I wish for is to be near him,
to glimpse his beloved face once again.

پتیاں لِکھاں مَیں شام نُوں

پتیاں لِکھاں مَیں شام نُوں ہَینوں پیا نظر نہ آوے
آنگن بنا ڈراؤنا، کِت بُدھ رَین وہاوے
پاندھے پنڈت جگت کے مَیں پُچھ رہی آں سارے
پوتھی بید کیا دوس ہَے جو اُلٹے بھاگ ہمارے
بھائیا وے جوتشیا! اِک سچی بات بھی کہیو
جے مَیں ہینی بھاگ دی، تم چُپ نہ رہیو
بھج سگاں تے بھج جاواں، سب رُت کے کراں فقیری
پر دُلڑی تُلڑی، چَولڑی ہَے گل وِچ پریم زنجیری
نیند گئی کِت دیس نُوں، اوہ بھی وَیرن میری
مَت سُفنے میں آن مِلے، اوہ نِیندر کیہڑی
رو رو جیو دلاندیاں غم کرنی آں دُوتا
نینوں نیر بھی نہ چلن، کسے کِیتا ٹُوٹا
ساجن تُمہری پیت سے مُجھ کو ہاتھ رکھ آیا
چھتر سُولاں سِرجھالیا پر تیرا پنتھ نہ پایا
پریم نگر چل وسیّے، جِتھے وَسّے کنت ہمارا
بُلّھیا! شَوہ توں منگتی ہاں جے دے دے نظارا

The Follower

What a dance your love has led me

since within me it opened its shop
and I drank from its poisoned cup.
Come to my help, apothecary.
What a dance your love has led me!

The sun has set; some redness remains.
Unveil your face but once again.
to the simpleton who set you free.
What a dance your love has led me!

I would not be denied. Now the boat
is in the whirlpool, barely afloat.
I chose to stay on, foolishly.
What a dance your love has led me!

تیرے عِشق نچائیاں

تیرے عِشق نچائیاں کر کے تھیّا تھیّا!
تیرے عِشق نے ڈیرا میرے اندر کیتا
بھر کے زہر پیالہ مَیں تاں آپے پیتا
جھب دے بُوہڑیں وے طبیبا نہیں تے مَیں مَر گیتا
تیرے عِشق نچائیاں کر کے تھیّا تھیّا!
چھُپ گیا وے سُورج، باہر رہ گئی آ لالی
وے مَیں صدقے ہوواں، دیویں مُڑ جے دِکھالی
پیرا! مَیں بھُل گیاں، تیرے نال نہ گیتا
تیرے عِشق نچائیاں کر کے تھیّا تھیّا!
ایس عشقے دے کولوں مَینوں ہٹک نہ مائے
لاہُو جاندڑے بیڑے کیہڑا موڑ لیائے
میری عقل جو بھُلّی نال مُھانیاں دے گیتا
تیرے عِشق نچائیاں کر کے تھیّا تھیّا!

Although it is a peacock's squawk
in the wild, this love is all I ask.
Inflicting this, why did you flee?
    What a dance your love has led me!

Love has brought me to the door
of Inayat, dressed like a whore.
I click my heels, and leap in glee.
    What a dance your love has led me!

ایس عشقے دی جھنگی وچ مور بولیندا
سانوں قبلہ تے کعبہ سوہنا یار دسیندا
سانوں گھائل کر کے پھیر خبر نہ لیتیا
تیرے عشق نچائیاں کر کے تھیّا تھیّا!

بُلھا! شوہ نے آندا مینوں عنایت دے بوہے
جس نے مینوں پوائے چولے سادے تے سُوہے
جاں میں ماری ہَے اڈی مل پیا ہَے وہیّا
تیرے عشق نچائیاں کر کے تھیّا تھیّا!

I'm in a Trap

I'm in a trap.

Love brought me to this fate;
just one glimpse was the bait.
Did my zeal deserve this blow?

I'm in a trap.

Take pity on my innocence
and give me some recompense.
This death is much too slow.

I'm in a trap.

Within touching distance yet
I cannot reach your heart.
Love me, or let me go.

I'm in a trap.

جند کڑکی دے مُنہ آئی

جِند کڑکی دے مُنہ آئی
عِشق تُہاڈا مَینوں دِسدا پُربت کولوں بھارا
اِک گھڑی دے دیکھن کارن چُک لیا ہر سارا
محنت مِلے کہ مِلدی ناہیں؟ ڈاہڈے دی اَشنائی
جِند کڑکی دے مُنہ آئی

پاکاں دا ہَے وَی وسیلہ، میرے تُسیں آپے ہووو
جِبھا گِدیاں، سنگ میرے جبا گو؛ سَونواں نالے سَونوو
جِس نے تَیں سنگ پِیت لگائی، کیہڑے سُکھ سوائی!
جِند کڑکی دے مُنہ آئی

جگ وِچ روشن نام تُہاڈا، عاشق توں کیوں نِدے ہو
وَسّو رِسّو وِچ بغل دے، اپنا بھیت نہ دَسدے ہو
اَدھکڑے وِچکاروں پھَڑکے مَیں اُلٹی لٹکائی
جِند کڑکی دے مُنہ آئی

Whatever You Touch

Whatever you touch takes on your hue.

Your eyes have caused a stir, unveil yourself
like the cloud-swept moon when it breaks through.

This dumbness is not a pose. For those who die
before death can strike them, their life renew.

Too many obstacles! Now take my hand
and help me over them as if I flew.

Dance, Bulleh, dance, your love has come to you.
Whatever you touch takes on your hue.

جو رنگ رنگیا گوہڑا رنگیا

جو رنگ رنگیا گوہڑا رنگیا، مُرشد والی لالی او یار
دُرِ معانی کی دھوم مچی ہے، نیناں تو گھُنڈ اُٹھالیں او یار
زُلف سیاہ وچ ہو یدِ بَیضا، اوہ چمکار دِکھالیں او یار

صُمٌ بُکمٌ عُمیٌ ہوئیاں، لائیاں دِی لَج پالیں او یار
مؤتُوا قَبلَ اَن تَمؤتُوا، موئی نوں پھیر جوالیں او یار

اوکھا جھیڑا عِشقے والا، سنبھل کے پیر ٹِکالیں او یار
ہَر شَے اندرٹوں آپے ہیں، آپے دیکھ دِکھالیں او یار

بُلھیا! شوہ گھر میرے آیا، کر کر ناچ دِکھالیں او یار
جو رنگ رنگیا گوہڑا رنگیا، مُرشد والی لالی او یار

Be Silent Now

Be silent now.

To the others truth is phlegm,
when you pass they raise their hem,
it brings out the beast in them,
for they would rather not know.

Truth wrecks the dogmatist's pride,
it gives the lover a bride
and a gay new world beside,
and says to the pilgrim, go.

But how can the lover be spare
of words, when he looks at her hair
and smells that scent-drenched air?
Renounce, renounce, take the vow.

Be silent now.

چُپ کر کے کریں گزارا

چُپ کر کے کریں گزارے نوں
سچ سُن کے لوک نہ سہندے نیں
سچ آکھیے تے گل پیندے نیں
پھر سچّے پاس نہ بہندے نیں
سچ مٹھا عاشق پیارے نوں

سچ شرع کرے بربادی اے
سچ عاشق دے گھر شادی اے
سچ کردا نویں آبادی اے
جیہا شرع طریقتہارے نوں

چُپ عاشق توں نہ ہُندی اے
جس آئی سچ سوگندی اے
جس ماہل سُہاگ دی گُندھی اے
چھڈ دُنیا، کوڑ پیارے نُوں
چُپ کر کے کریں گزارے نوں

Acquaintance

It is not acquaintance that I dread,
but the indifference to which it may lead.

بھروسا کیہ اشنائی دا

بھروسا کیہ اشنائی دا
ڈر لگدا بے پرواہی دا

Who's Keeping The Gossips Busy?

Who's keeping the gossips busy?
What ecstatic being is here
who is so drenched in oneness
for caste he has no care?
    Whose fame has caused such a din,
    who is nearer than your skin,
    who says I reside within,
    here, there, everywhere?
Shun the ground where untruths hiss,
receive love's hallowed kiss,
be where your beloved is,
and nothing else will matter.

چلو دیکھیے اوس مستانڑے نُوں

چلو دیکھیے اوس مَستانڑے نُوں
جدھی ترنجتاں دے وچ پئی اے دُھم
اوہ تے ئَ وَحدت وچ رنگدا اے
نہیں پُچھّدا "ذات دے کیہہ ہو تم؟"

جدھا شور چو پھیر پیا پَیندا اے
اوہ کول تیرے نِت رہندا اے
کے نَحنُ اَقرَبُ کہندا اے
کے آکھدا اے "فِی اَنفُسِکُم"

چھڈ جھوٹھ بھرم دی پَستی نُوں
کر عشق دی قائم مستی نُوں
گئے پہنچ سَجّن دی بستی نُوں
جو ہوئے عُمئ بُکمُ تے صُمّ

None owns these heaps of rubble,
life is nothing but trouble,
wayfarer, learn to ride double
with one giving care for care.
Bulleh Shah, take a cue,
whom you seek is seeking you,
blessings on all you do
if you surrender to His care.

نہ تیرا اے، نہ میرا اے

جگ فانی جھگڑا جھیڑا اے

بنا مُرشد رہبر کیہڑا اے

پڑھ: "فَانْذُكُرُونِیْ اَذْكُرْ كُمْ"

بُلّھے شاہ! اسے بات اشارے دِی

جنھاں لگّی تانگھ نظّارے دِی

دِس پَئی منزل وِنجھارے دِی

ہَے یَدُ اللّٰہ فَوْقَ اَیْدِیْكُمْ

The World's a Fun-Fair

The world's a fun-fair.

What did I do today? What of tomorrow?
A bad ploughing will only bring sorrow.

The world and my love mad me their slave.
But you'll go empty-handed to the grave.

Each in his turn youngster and old man fade,
innkeeper and servingman, mistress and maid.

To win his love, Bulleh exercises his wits;
first fashions a pot, then shatters it to bits.

Stroll through the bazar, join the revelry there,
then on to the next. The world's a fun-fair.

خَلق تماشے آئی یار

خَلق تماشے آئی یار!
اَج کِیہ کِیتا؟ کل کِیہ کرنا؟ بَھٹھ اساڈا آیا!
اَیسی واہ کِیاری بِیجی، چِپڑیاں کھیت وَنجایا

اِک اُلانھبا سیّاں دا ہَے، دُوجا ہَے سنسار
ننگے ناموُس اِتھوں دے اتتھے، لاہ پگڑی بھوئیں مار

نڈھا کِردا، بُڈھا کِردا، آپو اپنی واری
کِیہ بی بی، کِیہ باندی لوَنڈی، کِیہ دھوبن بھٹھیاری

بُلھاشوہ نوُں دیکھن جاوے، آپے بہانہ کردا
گوُنوگوُنی بھانڈے گھڑکے بٹھیکریاں کر دھردا

اسے تماشا دیکھ کے چِل پَو، اگلا دیکھ بازار
واہ وا چھنِج پَئی دربار، خَلق تماشے آئی یار!

With Love My Heart Overflows

With love my heart overflows.

Some girls are laughing and talking
and some are sadly walking.
That's the way it goes.

With love my heart overflows.

I was all dolled up for him
when he went off on a whim.
Now I'm fit for the crows.

With love my heart overflows.

That I'm so sad and ashamed
my eyes are to be blamed.
One look can heal God knows.

With love my heart overflows.

دِل لوچے مَاہی یار نُوں

دِل لوچے ماہی یار نُوں
اِک ہَس ہَس گلّاں کر دِیاں
اِک روندیاں دھوندیاں پھر دِیاں
کہو پُھلی بسنت بہار نُوں
دِل لوچے ماہی یار نُوں
مَیں کھاتی دھوتی رہ گئی
کوئی گنڈھ سَجن دِل سب گئی
بھاہ لاویے ہار سِنگار نُوں
دِل لوچے ماہی یار نُوں
مَیں دُوتیاں گھائل کیتی آں
سُولاں گھیر چوپھیروں لیتی آں
گھر آ ماہی دِیدار نُوں
دِل لوچے ماہی یار نُوں

The Broken Spinning-Wheel

The spinning-wheel is broken,
           I cannot spin.
Call the smith, for the axle
           wobbles on its pin.
The thread keeps breaking, smith,
           Let your job be neat;
it sways so that not a spool
           comes off complete.
I cannot tie it well, it slips
           again and again;
its grease is all used up,
           it creaks and groans.
The spinning-wheel is broken,
           I cannot spin.

How shall this long day pass
           till I can meet
my love? He is gone with the cows
           and my mind's feet
follow him to the pasture.
           The girls say come
and spin, but my heart is heavy,
           and hands numb.
Come back, love, come back again,
           my heart makes din,
reach out your arms to me
           and take me in.
The spinning-wheel is broken,
           I cannot spin.

ڈھلک گئی چرخے دی ہتّھی

ڈھلک گئی چرخے دی ہتّھی، کتّیا مُول نہ جباوے
تکلے نُوں وَل پَے پَے جاندے، کون لُہار سدا وے
تکلے توں وَل لاہیں لُہارا، تندی ٹُٹ ٹُٹ جباوے
گھڑی گھڑی اسے جھولے کھاندا، چھلّی اِک نہ لاہوے
پیتا نہیں جو بَیڑی بنھاں، بائِڑ ہتھ نہ آوے
چمڑیاں اُتّے چوپڑ نابیں، مابل پئی بڑلاوے
ڈھلک گئی چرخے دی ہتّھی، کتّیا مُول نہ جباوے

دن حِسرڑھیا کد گُزرے، مَینوں پیارا مُکھ دکھلاوے
ماہی چھڑ گیا نال مہیں دے، کتن کِس نُوں بھاوے
جِت یار اُتّے وَل اکھیاں، دِل میرا بیلے دھاوے
تنجن کتّن سدّن سیّاں، برہوں ڈھول وجباوے
عرض ایہو، مَینوں آن ملے ہُن، کون وسیلہ جباوے
سے مَتاں داکت لیا لبّھا، مَینوں شوہ گل لاوے
دن حِسرڑھیا کد گُزرے، مَینوں پیارا مُنہ دِکھلاوے

The Transformation

'Ranjha, Ranhja' I cried till only Ranjha is there?
I'm transformed, now Heer has disappeared.

We are synonymous: one heart, a single thought,
I am expunged, and Ranjha stands out clear.

Since he is inside me, he is all that exists,
that which I show to the world is just veneer.

Don the sackcloth, throw the white dress away,
for they are covered with stains who whiteness wear.

Hazara calls me, in Sial no friends are near.
'Ranjha, Ranjha' I cried till only Ranjha is here.

''رانجھا رانجھا'' کر دی

''رانجھا رانجھا''! کر دی ہُن مَیں آپے رانجھا ہوئی
سَدّو مَینوں ''دھیدو رانجھا''، ''ہیر'' سنہ آکھو کوئی

رانجھا مَیں وِچ، مَیں رانجھے وِچ، غیر خیال سنہ کوئی
مَیں نہیں، اوہ آپے ہے، اپنی آپے کرے دِلجوئی

جو کُجھ ساڈے اندر وَسے ذات اساڈی سوئی
جس دے نال مَیں ہیونگھ لگایا او ہو جیسی ہوئی

چِٹّی چادر لاہ سُٹ کُڑیے، پہن فقیراں لوئی
چِٹّی چادر داغ لگیسی، لوئی داغ سنہ کوئی

تخت ہزارے لَے چل بُلھیا، سیالیں مِلے سنہ ڈھوئی
''رانجھا رانجھا'' کر دی ہُن مَیں آپے رانجھا ہوئی

The Lover's Way

Merchants in mosque and monastery, thugs in the landlord's pay.
The lover alone goes his secret, inviolable way.

دھر مسال دھڑوائی وسدے

دھر مسال دھڑوائی وسدے، ٹھاکر دوارے ٹھگ

وچ مسیت کو سینتے رہندے، عاشق رہن الگ

Rituals

Fasting, pilgrimage, and the call
to prayer, love has drowned them all.
 Can any artifice survive
 when messages of love arrive?
 On the ears only its sounds fall.
  Fasting, pilgrimage, and the call
  to prayer, love has drowned them all.

The moment Love came toward
me, rituals went by the board.
Love, only love, was then to be seen,
over and under, around, between.
The loveless noticed nothing at all.
  Fasting, pilgrimage, and the call
  to prayer, love has drowned them all.

روزے حج نماز نی مائے

روزے، حج، نماز نی مائے

مَینوں پیا نے آݨ بُھلائے

جباں پیا دیاں خبراں پیّاں

مَنطق، نحو سِکھے بُھل گئیاں

اُس احمد دے تار بجائے

روزے، حج، نماز نی مائے

مَینوں پیا نے آݨ بُھلائے

جباں پیا میرے گھر آیا

بُھلّی مَینوں شرحِ وِقایہ

ہر مظہر وِچ اوہا وِسدا

اندر باہر جلوہ اِس دا

بُھلّے لوکاں خبر نہ کائے

روزے، حج، نماز نی مائے

مَینوں پیا نے آݨ بُھلائے

All Cotton-Bolls are White

All cotton-bolls are white.

Warp and woof, spindle and reel,
back and front, head and heel,
will end up in the one cloth
that will not last the night.

All cotton-bolls are white.

Khaddar and muslin, coarse or fine,
dress for ploughman, groom, divine,
issue from the self-same loom
no matter what the guise.

All cotton-bolls are white.

The bangles worn by girls, and rings
and bracelets and such adornings
are from the same silver beaten,
though hands are dark or light.

All cotton-bolls are white.

سَب اِکّو رنگ کپاہیں دا

سب اِکّو رنگ کپاہیں دا!

تاتی، تانا، پیٹا، نلیاں

پیٹھ، نڑا، تے چھّا چھلیاں

آپو اپنے نام جِتاوݨ

وکھو وکھّی جائیں دا

سب اِکّو رنگ کپاہیں دا

چوسی، پَینیسی، کھدّر، دھوتر

مَلمل، خاسا اِکا سُوتر

پُوݨی وِچوں باہر آوے

بھگوا بھیس لُگائیں دا

سب اِکّو رنگ کپاہیں دا

کُڑیاں ہتھیں چھاپاں چھلّے

آپو اپنے نام سَوئلے

سبھّا اِگّا چاندی آکھو

کنگݨ، چوڑا باہیں دا

سب اِکّو رنگ کپاہیں دا

The Buyer

A hundred merchants are here who tell
of rubies they have brought to sell.

Hearing them, I craved immediately
two for my ears so people could see.

Look at my foolishness, I who am
nothing, went off to buy a gem.

What was the price they asked? I cried
at pin-pricks, and they wanted my head.

The lowly should not reach for the sky.
A glass-bead is all they can buy.

سے ونجارے آئے

سے ونجارے آئے نی مائے، سے ونجارے آئے
لالاں دا اوہ ونج کریندے، ہو کا آکھ سنائے

سُنیا ہوکا، مَیں دل گُزری مَیں بھی لال لیاواں
اِک نے اِک کِتّاں وچ پاکے لوکاں نُوں دِکھلاواں

کچّی کچ، ویہاج نے جاناں، لال ویہاجن چلّی
پلّے خرچ نے، ساکھ نے کائی، دیکھو ہارت چلّی

جاں مَیں مُل اوٹھاں توں پُچھیا، مُل کرن اوہ بھارے
ڈھِٹھ سُوئی دا کدے نے کھاہدا، اوہ پُچھّن سِر بارے

جیہڑیاں گیّاں لال دیہاجن اوٹھاں سیس لُہائے
سے ونجارے آئے نی مائے، سے ونجارے آئے

Love Comes on Bright New Wings

Love comes on bright new wings.

I read love's book. Ever since,
mosques have made me wince.
Now I revel in precincts
echoing to a thousand strings.

Love comes on bright new wings.

Genuflexions night and day
have worn the knee-caps away.
God's not in Tirath or Mecca,
but in hearts where true love sings.

Love comes on bright new wings.

Scatter the rosary, spurn
ablutions and the prayer-mat burn,
for lovers they sigh and yearn
to taste prohibited things.

Love comes on bright new wings.

عِشق دِی نویوں نویں بہار

عِشق دِی نویوں نویں بہار

جہاں میَں سبق عشق دا پڑھیا

مسجد کولوں جیوڑا ڈریا

پُچھ پُچھ ٹھاکر دوارے وڑیا

جتھے وحدے ناد ہزار

عِشق دِی نویوں نویں بہار

وید فُتراناں پڑھ پڑھ تھکّے

سجدے کردیاں گھس گئے متھے

نہ رب تیرتھ، نہ رب مکّے

جس پایا تِس نُور انوار

عِشق دِی نویوں نویں بہار

پھُوک مُصلّے، بھن سُٹ لوٹا

نہ پھڑ تسبیح، عاصا سوٹا

عاشق کہندے دے دے ہوکا

ترک حلالوں، کھا مُردار!

عِشق دِی نویوں نویں بہار

Ranjha is one with his bride.
She looked for him far and wide,
but he had never left her side.
Knowing this, we know all things.

Love comes on bright new wings.

ہیر رانجھے دے ہوگئے میلے

بھلّی ہیر ڈھونڈیندی بیلے

رانجھن یار بغل وچ کھیلے

سُرت نہ رہیا، سُرت سنبھار!

عِشق دی نویوں نویں بہار

Enough of Learning, Friend

Enough of learning, friend.
One A can begin and end.

> You study night and day
> while life is ticking away,
> when all you need is an A.
> Enough of learning, friend,

> > enough of learning!

> The books you read and write
> reach up to such a height
> they've quite shut off the light.
> You know not where you wend,

> > enough of learning, friend.

عِلموں بَسّ کریں او یار

عِلموں بَس کرِیں او یار!
اِگّو الفّ ترے درکار
عِلم نہ آوے وِچ شُمار
جہاندی عُمر، نہیں اعتبار
اِگّو الف ترے درکار
علموں بَس کریں او یار

عِلموں بَس کرِیں او یار!
پڑھ پڑھ، لِکھ لِکھ لاویں ڈھیر
ڈھیر کِتاباں، چار چوپھیر
گِردے چانن، وِچ انھیر
پُچھو: ''راہ''؟ تے خبر نہ سار
عِلموں بَس کرِیں او یار!

The muezzin shatters the air
while you heap prayer on prayer
and sermons drip from your hair,
but to what end?

                  Enough of learning, friend.

Has this knowledge brought relief
or added grief to grief?
You nab the just, and the thief
you fail to apprehend.

                  Enough of learning, friend.

Such learning fools elevates
and some fresh bother creates,
is used to con illiterates,
make vows with false intent,

                  Enough of learning, friend.

پڑھ پڑھ نفل نماز گُزاریں

اُچیاں بانگاں چپاگھّاں ماریں

مِنبر تے چڑھ وعظ پُکاریں

کِیتا تَیْنوں علم خوار

عِلموں بَس کریں او یار!

عِلموں پِئے قضیے ہور

اَکھّاں والے اَنّھے کور

پِھر دے سادھ تے چھڈّن چور

عِلموں بَس کریں او یار!

پڑھ پڑھ شیخ مشائخ کہاویں

اُلٹے مَسلے گھروں بناویں

بے عِلماں نُوں لُٹ لُٹ کھاویں

جھوٹھے سچّے کریں اِقرار

عِلموں بَس کریں او یار!

Mullahs mug their way to power,
and now are judge and juror;
and avarice grows by the hour,
and straight to hell you wend.

                    Enough of learning, friend.

You dream up problems in a wink,
schism is your meat and drink,
beneath saintly garb you stink,
saying what you don't intend,

                    Enough of learning, friend.

When the bait of Love I cast,
slippery Truth was hooked at last;
and the griefs which held me fast
God's mercy made an end.

                    Enough of learning, friend!

پڑھ پڑھ مُلّاں ہوئے قاضی

اللہ عِلماں باجھوں راضی

ہووے حرص دِنوں دِن تازی

تَینوں کِیتا حِرص خوار

عِلموں بَس کریں او یار!

پڑھ پڑھ مَسلے پیا سُناویں

کھاٹا شَک شُبھے دا کھاویں

دسّیں ہور، تے ہور کماویں

اَندر کھوٹ، باہر سُچیار

عِلموں بَس کریں او یار!

جَد میں سبق عِشق دا پڑھیا

دریا دیکھ وحدت دا وَڑیا

گھُمن گھیراں دے وِچ اڑیا

شاہ عنایت لایا پار!

عِلموں بَس کریں او یار!

Stop the Spinning-Wheel, Girl

Stop the spinning-wheel, girl.
Gather the cloth, take off the reel, girl.
  Your wedding day
  is just a week away,
  yet you sing and play
  within a shell soon to be peeled, girl.
Stop the spinning-wheel, girl.
  If dowryless you leave
  how can you hope to please?
  Your spouse will grumble and grieve.
  Take heed from one who knows the deal, girl.
Stop the spinning-wheel, girl.

کتّ کُڑے، سَ وَت کُڑے

کتّ کُڑے، سَ وَت کُڑے
لاہ چھلّی، بھـروٹے گھتّ کُڑے
ماں پیوتیـرے گنڈھـیں پایاں
اَجے سَ تیُینوں سُرتاں آیاں
دِن تھوڑے تے چپا مُکایاں
سَ آئیں پیکے وَتّ کُڑے
کتّ کُڑے، سَ وَت کُڑے

جے داج وِہوتی جباویں گی
تاں کِسے بھلّی سَ بھاویں گی
تُوں شَوہ نوں کوِیں رِجھاویں گی
کُجھ اَے فقیراں دِی متّ کُڑے
کتّ کُڑے، سَ وَت کُڑے

Playmates who are wise
are busy with needle and dyes,
but you are set for a house
where you'll not get a square meal, girl.
Stop the spinning-wheel, girl.
When the groom meets you
he will look right through
the pretty face on view,
and how will you then feel, girl?
Stop the spinning-wheel, girl.
Gather the cloth, take off the reel, girl.

تیرے نال دِیاں داج رنگائے نی

اوکھاں سُوہے سالُو پائے نی

تُوں پیر اُلٹے کیوں چپائے نی

جا اوتھے لگسی تتّ کُتڑے

کتّ کُتڑے، نہ وَت کُتڑے

شَوہ، بلّھیا، گھر اپنے آوے

چوڑا بیٹرا تدے سُہاوے

گن ہوسی تاں گلے لگاوے

نہیں روسیں نئیں رتّ کُتڑے

کتّ کُتڑے، نہ وَت کُتڑے

لاہ چھلّی، بھروٹے گھتّ کُتڑے

Dogs are Better than You

You stay up all night to pray,
but dogs are sleepless too;

      they're better than you.

To bark and bark, and then to sleep
on the first trash-heap you view;

      they're better than you.

They will not leave their master's house
though beaten black and blue;

      they're better than you.

Bulleh, you'd better mend your ways,
else it will be proved true:

      dogs are better than you.

كُتّے تیتھوں اُتّے

راتیں جاگیں، کریں عبادت
راتیں جاگن کُتّے تیتھوں اُتّے

بھونکن توں بند مُول نہ ہندے
جا روڑی تے سُتّے: تیتھوں اُتّے

خصم اپنے دا دَر نہ چھڈ دے
بھانویں وجّن جُتّے: تیتھوں اُتّے

بلّھے شاہ! کوئی رخت ویہاج لے
نہیں تے بازی لے گئے کُتّے
تیتھوں اُتّے

Names

Having understood, why heed the storm
over such names as Allah and Ram.

گل سمجھ لئی تے رولا کِیہ

گل سمجھ لئی تے رولا کِیہ
اے رام، رحیم تے مَولا کِیہ؟

Come See Me Once in a While

Come see me once in a while.

You are gone, friend, far away
beyond my reach. Many a day
Kasur has missed your smile.

Come see me once in a while.

Now hell has opened its bogs.
Punjab has gone to the dogs.
This hell is the nethermost hell.

Come see me once in a while.

A brief visit now and then
will give some ease to my pain.
This century cramps our style.

Come see me once in a while.

The flames engulfing my house,
Bulleh, only love can douse.
Inayat calls up the aisle

Come see me once in a while.

گَدی آمِل یار پیاریا!

دُور و دُور اساتھوں گئیوں

اصلاتے جا کے بہ رہئیوں

کیوں قصر قصُور وِساریا

گَدی آمِل یار پیاریا

در کھُلّا حَشر عذاب دا

بُرا حَال ہویا پنجاب دا

وِچ ہاوِیے دوزخ ساڑیا

گَدی آمِل یار پیاریا

کدیں آویں وڈھ پرواریا

تیرے دُکھاں سَانوں ماریا

مُنّہ بارہویں صدی پیاریا

گَدی آمِل یار پیاریا

بُلّھا! شَوہ میرے گھر آوسی

میری بلدی بھاہ بُجھاوسی

عِنایت دَم دَم نال چِتاریا

گَدی آمِل یار پیاریا

Lass, Look to Your Spinning

Lass, look to your spinning.

Mother scolds you every day,
but your mind is far away;
you keep modesty at bay;
when will you understand?

Lass, look to your spinning.

So much advice I hurl
each day at this silly girl;
she will be in a whirl
when bad times are at hand.

Lass, look to your spinning.

کرکتّن وَل دھیان کُڑے

کرکتّن وَل دھیان کُڑے!
نِت مَتّیں دیندی ما، دِھیا!
کیوں پھرنی ایں اَینویں آ ـ دِھیا!
نہ شرم حیا نُوں گوا دِھیا!
تُوں کدے تاں سمجھ نداں کُڑے
کرکتّن وَل دھیان کُڑے
نِت مَتّیں دِیاں، وَلّی نُوں
اِسّ بھولی، کملی، جھلّی نُوں
جد پَوسی وخت اِکّلی نُوں
تد ہا! ہا! کرسی جہان کُڑے
کرکتّن وَل دھیان کُڑے

The new cotton crop is in.
Take it for scouring, and then
sit down to spin and spin,
or spinning time will be gone.

  Lass, look to your spinning.

Here you do not belong,
so now switch off this song,
or you will lose the chance
to set up house on your own.

  Lass, look to your spinning.

What you get under this roof
topped with a fond mother's love,
will be lost soon enough.
A tough mother-in-law waits.

  Lass, look to your spinning.

اَج گھر وِچ نویں کپاہ گُڑے

تُوں جھب جھب ویلنا ڈاہ گُڑے

رُوں ویل، پنجھاوَن جاہ گُڑے

پھیر کل نہ تیرا جان گُڑے

کرکتّن وَل دھیان گُڑے

ایہ پَیکا راج دِن چار گُڑے

نہ کھیڈو کھیڈ گزار گُڑے

نہ وھلی روہ کر کار گُڑے

گھر بار نہ کر ویران گُڑے

کرکتّن وَل دھیان گُڑے

تُوں سدا نہ پیکے رہتا اے

نہ پاس اَمڑی دے بہنا اے

بھا! انت وچھوڑا سہتا اے

وسّ پسَیں گی سسّ ہناں گُڑے

کرکتّن وَل دھیان گُڑے

The sun is high. Attend
to your chores, and send
the dowry to the dyer, then
you'll have earned each one's respect.

Lass, look to your spinning.

You think that you are fair,
take pride in your silken hair,
but who will heed it there?
These will be gone in a trice.

Lass, look to your spinning.

A time is coming soon
when you'll be left alone,
then help there will be none
till you call on Bulleh's guide.

Lass, look to your spinning.

کت لَے نی کُجھ، کتا لَے نی

ہُن تاݨی تند اُنا لَے نی

تُوں اپنا داج رنگا لَے نی

تُوں تد ہوسیں پَر دھیان گُڑے

کرکتّݨ وَل دھیان گُڑے

کر مان نہ حُسن جوانی دا

پردیس نہ رہن سیلانی دا

اس دُنیا جھُوٹھی فانی دا

نہ رہسی نام نشان گُڑے

کرکتّݨ وَل دھیان گُڑے

اک اَوکھا ویلا آوے گا

سب ساک سَیݨ بھجّ جاوے گا

کر مَدّد پار لنگھاوے گا

اوہ بُلھے دا سُلطان گُڑے

کرکتّݨ وَل دھیان گُڑے

This Mad Lover

What does this mad lover do? you ask.
He shuttles between temple and mosque.

He is one, but one among many because
there are no secrets in a crowded house.

Everywhere he is seen, each place his own,
for in the stream of oneness none may drown.

Bulleh, love devours all, takes all to task.
What does this mad lover do? you ask.

کوئی پُچھّو دِلبر کِیہ کردا

کوئی پُچھّو ''دِلبر کِیہ کردا؟ اسے جو کردا سو کردا'' !

وِچ مسِیت نماز گزارے، بُت خانے جا وَڑدا

آپے اِتّو، کئی لکھ گھراں دے، مالک ہے گھر گھر دا

اِکسے گھر وِچ رَسدے وَسدے نہیں رہندا وِچ پَردا

جِت وَل دیکھاں اُت وَل اوہو، ہر دی سنگت کردا

وحدت دے دریا دے اندر سب جگ دِسّے تَردا

بُلّھیا! شوہ دا عِشق بگھیلا، رَت پِیندا گوشت چَردا

کوئی پُچھّو ''دِلبر کِیہ کردا؟ اسے جو کردا سو کردا'' !

Penitence

What sort of penitence is this?

That sits on the lips, but has no place in the heart,
and yet expects to be granted bliss;

whose name is Muslim, but whose furtive eyes
look for lacunas; whose ambitions hiss;

whose heart is absent when the hand is placed
on the Holy Book in solemn promise.

O ruthless ones, the trap you set for others,
is set for you. Be sure it will not miss.

What sort of penitence is this?

کیسی توبہ

کیسی توبہ ہے اے توبہ، ایسی توبہ نہ کر یار

مُونہوں توبہ، دِلوں نہ کردا، اِس توبہ تھیں ترک نہ پھڑدا
کِس غفلت نے پایو پردا، تَینوں بخشے کیوں غفّار

سانوں دے کے لَویں سوائے، ڈُھڈیاں اُتّے بازی لائے
مُسلمانی اوہ کِتھوں پائے جس دا ہووے ایہہ کِردار

جِت نہ جانا اوتھے جاویں، حق بیگانہ مُکّر کھاویں
کُوڑ کِتاباں برتے چپاویں ہووے کیہ تیرا اعتبار

ظالم ظلموں نہیں ڈر دے، اپنی کیتیوں آپے مَردے
نہیں خوف خُدا دا کردے، اِتھے اوتھے ہووِن خوار

کیسی توبہ ہے اے توبہ، ایسی نہ کر یار

Who Choose Cold-Hearted Dears

Who choose cold-hearted dears
must learn to cope with tears.

> Now he is gone
> heart from body is drawn,
> in its place is a stone.
> To advice you turned deaf ears.
> > Who choose cold-hearted dears.

> You trust, you fool,
> one with no pity at all,
> who laughs when sparrows fall,
> and claps his hands and jeers.
> > Who choose cold-hearted dears.

> He has betrayed
> every promise he made,
> but I still wait and wait,
> undeterred by his sneers.

Who choose cold-hearted dears
must learn to cope with tears.

کِیہ بیدَرداں دے سنگے یاری!

کِیہ بیدردِاں دے سنگے یاری!
روون اَکھیاں زار و زاری
ساؤں گئے بیدردی چھڈ کے
سِینے سانگے ہجر دی گڈ کے
جِسموں جِندڑوں لے گئے کڈ کے
اے گل کر گئے ہیںیاری
کِیہ بیدردِاں دے سنگے یاری!

بیدردِاں دا کِیہ بھرواسا
خَوف نہِیں دِل اَندّر ماسا
چپڑیاں مَوت، گنواراں ہاسا
مَگروں ہس ہس تاڑی ماری
کِیہ بیدردِاں دے سنگے یاری!

آون کہ، گئے، پھیر نہ آئے
آون دے سب قول بھُلائے
مَیں بھُلّی، بھُل نَیں لگائے
کیہ ملے سن ٹھگ بیوپاری
کِیہ بیدردِاں دے سنگے یاری!
روون اَکھیاں زار و زاری

My Love has Come to Call

Stop the clock on the wall
for my love has come to call.

Each swift minute is a bite
into the span of the night.
If they knew my plight.
the minute hands would fall.

My love has come to call.

Sweet music adds its boon
to a sweet singer in tune.
Now prayer and fast are done.
for the cup is raised in skoal.

My love has come to call.

گھڑیالی دیو نِکال نی

گھڑیالی دیو نِکال نی
اَج پی گھر آیا لال نی

گھڑی گھڑی گھڑی گھڑیال بجاوے
رَین وَصل دِی پِیا گھٹاوے
میرے من دِی بات جے پاوے
ہتھوں چپا سُٹّے گھڑیال نی
       گھڑیالی دیو نِکال نی

انحد باجا بجے سُہانا
مُطرِب! شگھڑا تان ترانا
بھُلا صَوم، صلاۃ دوگانہ
مدھ پیالہ دین کلال نی
       گھڑیالی دیو نِکال نی

Just one glimpse can fetch
delight to the meanest wretch.
To make this short night stretch
against time throw up a wall.

    My love has come to call.

To entice him I did use
all sorts of spells and brews.
May he, now he's in the house,
stay a million years in all.

    My love has come to call.

Bulleh, what is my life
unless love twists its knife?
He's come after so much strife
now may no misfortune befall.

    My love has come to call.

دُکھ دِلّدر اُٹھ گیا سارا
مُکھ دیکھاں تے عجب نظارا
رَین ودھی، کچھ کرو پسارا
دِن اَگّے دھرو دیوال نی
گھڑیالی دیو نِکال نی

ٹونے کامن کیے بِتیرے
سہرے آئے وڈ وڈیرے
تاں جانی گھر آیا میرے
رَانجھ لکّھ ورھے اُس نال نی
گھڑیالی دیو نِکال نی

بلّھیا! شَوہ دِی سچّ پیاری
نی مَیں تار نہارے تاری
کوِیں کوِیں مِری آئی واری
ہُن وِچھڑن ہویا مُحال نی
گھڑیالی دیو نِکال نی
اَج پی گھر آیا لال نی

Up With Your Veil, Love

Up with your veil, love,
and look at me.

I'm immune to the smears
on my character. My dear,
the harder they jeer
the louder my ecstasy.

Up with your veil, love,
and look at me.

Let my prayer be heard.
Love, say a word.
How can a bird
be blithe sans its tree?

Up with your veil, love,
and look at me.

گھونگٹ اوھلے نہ لُک سجنا!

گھونگٹ اوھلے نہ لُک سجنا

مَیں مُشتاق دِیدار دی ہاں!

تیرے باجھ دِیوانی ہوئی

ٹوکاں کر دے لوک سہوئی

جیکر یار کریں دِلجوئی

تاں فریاد پُکار دی ہاں

گھونگٹ اوھلے نہ لُک سجنا

مَیں مُشتاق دِیدار دی ہاں!

مُفت وِکاندی جاندی باندی

مِل ماہی جند اَینویں جاندی

اِک دَم ہجر نہیں مَیں ساہندی

بُلبُل مَیں گلزار دی ہاں

گھونگٹ اوھلے نہ لُک سجنا

مَیں مُشتاق دِیدار دی ہاں!

Clay

The horse is clay; and so is the rider—
how strangely clay runs after clay,

    that's its way.

And clay kills clay with a clay sword;
the more clayey one will be the one to slay,

    that's its way.

What's the garden but clay? And its flowers?
Clay has come to it in a season of clay,

    that's its way.

Four elements spin the world, but a fifth
overrules them, while the rest betray;

    that's their way.

مَاٹی وتدم کریندی یار

مائی جوڑا، مائی گھوڑا، مائی دا اسوار
مائی نُوں مائی دوڑائے، مائی دا کھڑکار
مائی وتدم کریندی یار!
مائی نُوں مائی مارن لگی، مائی دا ہتھیار
جس مائی پر بِہُستی مائی، تِس مائی ہنکار
مائی وتدم کریندی یار!
مائی باغ، بغیچہ مائی، مائی دی گلزار
مائی نُوں مائی دیکھن آئی، مائی دی اے بہار
مائی وتدم کریندی یار!
چار سیاں رَل کھیڈن لگیاں، پنجویں وِچ سردار
ہس کھیڈ مُڑ مائی ہویاں، پوندیاں پیر پسار
مائی وتدم کریندی یار!

The Benighted

Mullah and torch-bearer come of one stock,
giving light to others, themselves in the dark.

مُلّاں تے مشالچی

مُلّاں تے مشالچی دُوݨھاں اِکّو چِت
لوکاں کر دے چانتا، آپ انھیرے وِچ

I'm Harbouring a Thief

I'm harbouring a thief.
Since he wears my guise how can I give him away?
If he tiptoes out there will be hell to pay.
I'm harbouring a thief.

Some will understand, others will scratch their head.
Will the pother end if he's not the one they expect?
I'm harbouring a thief.

The rulers of Lahore under threatening skies
put their hands to their ears and shut their eyes.
I'm harbouring a thief.

میری بُکّل دے وِچ چور!

ہری بُکّل دے وِچ چوراِنی، ہری بُکّل دے وِچ چور

سا دھو کس نُوں ٹوک سُناواں: ہری بُکّل دے وِچ چور
چوری چوری نِکل گیا تے جگ وِچ پَے گیا شور
ہری بُکّل دے وِچ چور
جس جا تا تِس جبان لیا، تے ہور ہوئے جُھر مور
چُک گئے سارے جھگڑے جھیڑے، نِکل پیا کوئی ہور
ہری بُکّل دے وِچ چور
عرش منوّر بانگاں مِلیاں، سُنیاں تخت لہور
شاہ عنائت کُنڈیاں پائیاں، لگ چُھپ چُھپ کھِجدا ڈور
ہری بُکّل دے وِچ چوراِنی، ہری بُکّل دے وِچ چور

Gather Round Me, Friends

Gather round me, friends, my stay here is done.
I'm off to the house where you'll join me soon.

What was my dowry? A stove and a shawl.
When I think of it now the tear-drops fall.
Like a lost crane I'll roam when I leave you all.

So many arrows of pain that struck home
deck the body, but what of those to come?
They will sneer at me there; this is my doom.

All must go, of remission not a word.
Who am I, when my betters were not spared?
Only the righteous will get bed and board.

Gather round me, friends, my stay here is done.
I'm off to the house where you'll join me soon.

مِل لؤ سہیلڑ یو

مِل لؤ سہیلڑ یو، میری راج گہیلڑ یو، مَیں ساہوریاں گھر جاݨا
تُاں بھی ہوسی اللہ بھاݨا، مَیں ساہوریاں گھر جاݨا
امّاں بابل داج جو دِتّا: اِک چولی اِک چُنّی
داج تِنھاں دا دیکھ کے ہُن مَیں ہنجو بھر بھر رُئّی
اِک وچھوڑا سیّاں دا، جویں ڈاروں کُونج وچھُنّی

رنگ برنگے سُول اپُٹھّے جاندے چیریں جی نُوں
ایتھوں دے دُکھ نال لجاواں، اگلے سونہپاں کیہنوں
سّس سِناناں دیوݨ طعنے بڑی نموشی مَینوں

ایتھے سانوں رہݨ سہ مِلدا، جاݨا واروواری
چنگ چنگیرے پکڑ منگالے، مَیں کیہ دی پنہاری؟
جس گٹن پلّے، بول سَوتّے، سوئی شوہ نُوں پیاری

مِل لؤ سہیلڑ یو، میری راج گہیلڑ یو، مَیں ساہوریاں گھر جاݨا
تُاں بھی ہوسی اللہ بھاݨا، مَیں ساہوریاں گھر جاݨا

Truth Will Out

Truth will out

     though it adds fuel to fire.
     Lies are a burnt-out pyre.
     So after looking at both
          the tongue must shout,
          truth will out.

     In the darkness walk with care
     for floors are slippery here.
     Ascertain who is within.
          while others hunt without.
          Truth will out.

     Who knows what the sadhu knows
     will surely find repose.
     On the tideless river of peace
          he is afloat.
          Truth will out.

مُنہ آئی بات نہ رہندی اے

سَچ کہواں تے بھانبڑ مَچدا اے

جھوٹھ آکھیاں کُجھ نہ بَچدا اے

جی دوہاں گلاں توں بَچدا اے

چَچ چَچ کے جیبھا کہندی اے

مُنہ آئی بات نہ رہندی اے

اسیں تِلکن بازی ویہڑا اے

تھم تھم کے ٹُرو اندھیرا اے

وَڑ اندر دیکھو کیہڑا اے

کیوں خلقت باہر ڈھونڈیندی اے

مُنہ آئی بات نہ رہندی اے

جس پایا بھیت قلندر دا

راہ کھوجیا اپنے اندر دا

اوہ واسی ہے سُکھ مندر دا

جِتھے کوئی نہ چڑھدی لہندی اے

مُنہ آئی بات نہ رہندی اے

Whatever the time and place
God is in every face.
Unalterable this fact
     covert or not.
      Truth will out.

The lessons experience taught
have all been dearly bought.
The rest is a stream's babble
     not worth a thought.
      Truth will out.

Love, Bulleh, is part of us
without which is nothing but fuss.
If only we had the eyes
     we would not doubt.
      Truth will out.

اِک لازِم شرطِ اُدب دی اے
سانُوں بات معلُومی سَب دی اے
ہر ہر وِچ صُورت رَبّ دی اے
کتے ظاہر، کتے چُھپیندی اے
مُنہ آئی بات نہ رہندی اے

اَساں پڑھیا علمِ تحقیقی اے
اوتھے اِکّو حَرف حقیقی اے
ہور جھگڑا سب وِھیکی اے
ایویں رولا پا پا بہندی اے
مُنہ آئی بات نہ رہندی اے

شَوہ لُبّھا! ساں تھِیں وَکّھ نہیں
بِت شوہ دے دُوجا کَکّھ نہیں
پر دیکھن والی اَکّھ نہیں
تہِنیں جان جُدایاں سہندی اے
مُنہ آئی بات نہ رہندی اے

God has Come Down as Man

God has come down as man.

> He is deer and leopard, kills and is killed,
> he is master and slave, sells and is sold.

God has come down as man.

> I am a puppet on a string, and such
> is his control, I tremble at a touch.

God has come down as man.

مَولا آدمی بَن آیا

مولا آدمی بَن آیا

آپے آہو، آپے چِیتا، آپے مارِن دھایا
آپے صاحِب، آپے بردا، آپے مُسل وِکایا
مَولا آدمی بَن آیا

بازیگر کِیہ بازی کھیڈی، مَینوں پُتلی وانگ نچایا
مَیں اُس تالی پر نچّاں ہاں جو گِت مت یار لکھایا
مَولا آدمی بَن آیا

I'm Waiting

I'm waiting, pass this way once more,
Enayat Shah, my eyes are sore
with looking for you at the door.

    I'm waiting, pass this way once more.

Who will lead me to the place
of my master, so by his grace
he may my heart and body restore.

    I'm waiting, pass this way once more.

See, I am dressed to the nines
for that cold man. I see no signs
of him, and am stricken to the core.

    I'm waiting, pass this way once more.

Bulleh, every beat of your heart
cries love, but the tears start
to the eyes when they see what's in store.

    I'm waiting, pass this way once more.

مَیں اُڈیکاں کر رہی

مَیں اُڈیکاں کر رہی، گدی آ، کر پھیرا
چشماں سچ وِچھائیاں، دِل کیتا وِہڑا
تُوں لٹکیندا آوڑیں شاہ عنایت میرا
مَیں اُڈیکاں کر رہی، گدی آ، کر پھیرا

اوہ اجیہا کون ہے جبا آکھے جیہڑا
مَیں وِچ کیے تقصیر ہے، مَیں بردا تیرا
تَیں باجھوں مرا کون ہے، دِل ڈھاس نہ میرا
مَیں اُڈیکاں کر رہی، گدی آ، کر پھیرا

ہَتھ کنگن، بانھ چُوڑیاں، گل نو رنگ چولا
ماہی مَینوں کر گیا کوئی راول رولا
جَل بَل ڈھائیں ماریاں، دِل پتھر تیرا
مَیں اُڈیکاں کر رہی، گدی آ، کر پھیرا

بُلّھیا! شوہ دے واسطے دل بھڑکت بھائیں
اوکھا پَینڈا پریم دا، دُکھ گھٹدا ناہیں
دِل وِچ دَھکے جھیڑ دے، ہر دھائیں میرا
مَیں اُڈیکاں کر رہی، گدی آ، کر پھیرا

I'm Just a Sweepress

I'm just a sweepress.

Hair uncombed, barefoot, I receive word
of his coming, and am left perturbed.
The broom my meditation: with it I've swept
into my basket all that the world has kept.
The judge knows much, the king rules with fear,
but I'm happy to be allowed in here.

I'm just a sweepress.

Being untouchable, none comes near
me, but I'm on the way, I do not care.
What's my pay after a hard day's grind?
A hard pillow, and what you leave behind.
This is my life: cold and sickness and scorn;
an empty stomach, clothes that are torn.
The straws of my broom are all that own.

I'm just a sweepress.

مَیں چُوہڑھیڑی آں

مَیں چُوہڑھیڑی آں سچّے صاحِب دے درباروں
پیروں ننگی، سِروں جھنڈولی، سُنہیا آیا پاروں
تڑبراٹ کُجھ بندا ناہیں، کِیہہ لَیساں سنساروں
دھیان کی چھیلی، گیان کا جھاڑو، کام کرودھ نِت جھاڑوں
پکڑاں چھجلی، حرص اُڈاواں، چھٹّاں مالگزاروں
وتاضی جبانے، حاکم جبانے، فارغخطی بیگاروں
رات دِنیں مَیں ایہو منگدی: دُور سنے کر دربارو
مَیں چُوہڑھیڑی آں سچّے صاحِب دے دربارو
کیا چُوہڑی، کیا ذات چُوہڑی دی، ہرکوئی ساتوں نتّے
کر کار بیگار ارتھیا، ہونا جباں پر سائِیں وسّے
رِکیہہ کُجھ پڑتی، لاگے چُوہڑی دا، گُھنڈی اور سرہانا
جو کُجھ دِتّا آپ سائِیں نے سوگھر لَے کے جبانا
پھٹا پُرانا بھاگے اساڈا، بھٹکھ، ٹُکڑ: سچ، بیہہ
فاقہ کڑاکا، منگن بِنن، چپال اساڈی ایہہ
رچھ رچھوڑتے تیلے کانے ایے اساڈی کاروں
مَیں چُوہڑھیڑی آں سچّے صاحِب دے دربارو

The Load

What I've picked up costs me dear.

> Its thorns are sharp, my clothes are torn,
> I must deal with one cold to the bone,
> his servants tax each stick I own
> which is quite a bundle. As soon
> as it is tied, the merchants will be here.

> What I've picked up costs me dear.

The slope is steep, and heavy the load
on my head, and I stumble on the road.
My misspent life tells on my face,
I am so weak and lacking in grace,
not Bulleh, but Inayat must steer.

> What I've picked up costs me dear.

مَیں کُسُنبا چُن چُن ہاری

مَیں کُسُنبا چُن چُن ہاری

اِیس کُسُنب دے حنار بھلیرے! اڑ اڑ چُنّی پاڑی
اِیس کُسُنب دا حاکم کرڑا، ظالم ہے پٹواری
اِیس کُسُنب دے چپار مُقدّم، مَلبہ منگدے بھاری
ہور ناں چگیا پھویا پھویا، بھر لئی مَیں پٹیاری
چُگ چُگ کے جو ڈھیری کیتا، آن لتھے بیوپاری

اوکھی گھاٹی مُشکل پَینڈا، سرتے گٹھڑی بھاری
عملاں والیاں سَب لنگھ گئیاں، رہ گئی او گٹھہاری
ساری عُمرا کھیڈ گوائی اوڑک بازی ہاری
مَیں کمین کُچی، کوجی، بے گُٹ کوٹ وچاری
بُکھا شوہ دے لائق ناہیں، شاہ عنایت تاری
مَیں کُسُنبا چُن چُن ہاری

From the First Moment

From the first moment love
has put me to the proof.

> He tossed me in the frying-pan,
> and tosses me over again.

> Not satisfied with my death,
> he kills with every breath.

> One ember on the body
> spread till it engulfed me.

> Bulleh, love will not settle
> for less, your most is little.

From the first moment love
has put me to the proof.

مَینوں لگڑا عشق

مَینوں لگڑا عِشق اَوَلڑا

اوّل دا، روز اَزل دا

وِچ کڑاہی تِل تِل پاوے

تلیاں نُوں چا تلدا

مویاں نُوں اے وَل وَل مارے

دلیاں نُوں چا دلدا

کیا جباناں کوئی چنگا لِکھی اے

نِت سُول کلیجے سِل دا

بُلّھا! شوہ دا نِیوں انوکھا

اوہ نہیں رلایاں رلدا

مَینوں لگڑا عِشق اَوَلڑا

اوّل دا، روز اَزل دا

Strange are the Ways of my Love

Strange are the ways of my love!

> To sleep I have kissed goodbye;
> on the roof I mope and sigh
> while mirages green my eye.
> No peace in city or grove.
>
> To glimpse is to die. One look
> and the noose is round your neck.
> I should have kept it in check,
> but Lahore's thug covered his bluff.

Strange are the ways of my love!

وَاہ وَارَمـــزِ سَجَّنْ دِی

واہ وا، رَمـــزِ سَجَّنْ دی ہور!

کوٹھے تے چَپَڑھ دیواں ہوکا
عِشق وِہاجو کوئی نـــ لوکا
اِسں دا مُول نہ کھائا دھوکا
جنگل، بَستی بیلے نہ ٹھور

دے دِیدار ہویا حَبد راہی
اَچن چیت پئَی گل پَہائی
ڈاہڈی کمیسی بے پَرواہی
مَینوں مِلیا ٹھگ لاہور
واہ وا، رَمـــزِ سَجَّنْ دی ہور!

Lovers walk silently where
is nobody else, and they stare
through the bars of silken hair,
strength from their limbs drained off.

Bulleh, what can you hope to find
when love is totally blind?
It is just a state of mind
that knows nor smooth nor rough.

Strange are the ways of my love!

عاشق پھردے چُپ چپاتے
جیسے مَست سدا، مدھ ماتے
دامِ زُلف دے اَندر پھاتے
اوتھے چلّے وَس نہ زور

بُلّھیا! شَوہ نُوں کوئی نہ دیکھے
جو دیکھے سو کہے نہ لیکھے
اُس دا رنگ، نہ رُوپ، نہ ریکھ اے
اوہی ہووے ہو کے چور

واہ واہ، رَمز سجن دی ہور!

Neither Hindu Nor Muslim

Neither Hindu nor Muslim
I sit with all on a whim.
Having no caste, sect, or creed,
I am different indeed.
Neither thirsty nor quite slaked,
I am not dressed nor naked.
I do not laugh, do not cry,
and neither stay nor go by.
I am not sinner or saint
knowing nor sin nor restraint.
Bulleh tries hard to shirk
the embrace of Hindu and Turk.

ہندُو نہیں، نہ مُسلمان

ہندُو نہیں، نہ مُسلمان   بہنے ترنجن، تج ابھّاں
سُنّی نہ، نہیں ہم شیعا   صلح کُل کا مارگ لیّا
بھکّھے نہ، نہیں ہم رجّے   ننگے نہ، نہیں ہم کجّے
روندے نہ، نہیں ہم ہسدے   اُجڑے نہ، نہیں ہم وسدے
پاپی نہ، سُدھری ناں   پاپ پُن کی راہ نہ جباں

بُلھّے شاہ! جو ہر چِت لاگے
ترک اور ہندو دوجن تیاگے

Obfuscation

Talk only of God, the rest is merely chatter,
though scholar and priest have tried to confuse the matter.

ہور نیں سبھے گلڑیاں

ہور نیں سبھے گلڑیاں، اللہ اللہ دی گل

کُجھ رولا پایا عالماں، کُجھ کاغذاں پایا جھلّ

The Semi-Literate

From the semi-literate I run, oh how I run!
for they are the biggest fools under the sun.
From the semi-literate I run, oh how I run!

پاپڑھیاں توں ندا ہاں میں

پاپڑھیاں توں ندا ہاں مَیں، پاپڑھیاں توں ندا ہاں!
عالمِ فاضل میرے بھائی، پاپڑھیاں میری عقل گوائی
پاپڑھیاں توں ندا ہاں مَیں، پاپڑھیاں توں ندا ہاں!

The Story of Creation

I've tracked the beauty down
which was the talk of the town.

A Word existed in space
which had no form or face.
None mighty or small.
No God or prophet at all.

I've tracked the beauty down
which was the talk of the town.

The Word had no sire or heir,
it was beyond compare.
It had no colour or smell.
There was no heaven or hell.

I've tracked the beauty down
which was the talk of the town.

Then the Word was mated
and angels and saints created
to choir around His seat,
and kneel at His feet.

I've tracked the beauty down
which was the talk of the town.

ہُن مَیں لِکھیا سوہنا یار

جدوں اَحد اِک اِکلّا سی، نہ ظاہر کوئی تجلّا سی
نہ ربّ رسُول نہ اللہ سی، نہ سی جبّارتے نہ قہّار

بے چُون و بے چُگوں سی، بے شبہ تے بے نمونہ سی
نہ کوئی رنگ نمُونہ سی، ہُن ہو یا گُونا گُون ہزار

پھر "کُن" کیہا "فیکُون" کمایا، بے چُونی تو چُون بنایا
"آحد" دے وِچ "میم" رلایا، تاہیوں کِیتا ایڈ پسار

ہُن مَیں لِکھیا سوہنا یار، جس دے حُسن دا گرم بزار

پیر پیغمبر اُس دے بردے، اِنس ملائک سجدے کردے
سر قدماں دے اُتّے دھر دے، سب توں وَڈی اوہ سرکار

And God was temple and mosque
and all you could ask,
but cold to fast and prayer-call.
He was above them all.

I've tracked the beauty down
which was the talk of the town.

Only the proper guide
can lead you to His side;
and unless you choose
Inayat, you will lose.

I've tracked the beauty down
which was the talk of the town.

تجوں مسيت تجوں بُت خانہ، برتی رہاں سنے روزہ جباتاں

بھُلا وضُو ، نماز دوگانہ، تَیں پَر جان کراں نِثار

جو کوئی اُس نُوں لکھیا چپا ہے، بے وسیلے سنے لکھیا جائے

شاہ عِنایت بھیت بتائے، تائیں کھُلّے سب اسرار

ہُن مَیں لکھیا سوہنا یار، جس دے حُسن دا گرم بزار

Love's Arrival

You came and I had to fall.
But why did you come at all?

Abraham set alight,
Zachariah sawn in half,
Joseph was auctioned off.
And what will be my lot?

You came and I had to fall.
But why did you come at all?

Sanaan made to feed swine,
Shams was skinned alive,
Mansur crucified.
Now I must toe the line.

کیوں عشقِ اَساں تے آیا اے

کیوں عشقِ اَساں تے آیا اے؟
توں آیا تے مَیں پایا اے

اِبراھیم چپا چھے سٹائیو
زکریے سر کلو تر دھرائیو
یُوسف ہٹو ہٹ وکائیو
کہو سانوں کیہہ لیایا اے
کیوں عشقِ اَساں تے آیا اے؟
توں آیا تے مَیں پایا اے

شیخ صنعان توں خوک چرائیو
شمس دی کھل اُلٹ لہائیو
سُولی تے منصور چڑھائیو
کر ہتھ ہُن کیں ول دھایا اے

You came and I had to fall.
But why did you come at all?

Whatever house you tried
was burnt to the ground;
on the ash-heap you were found.
Are you now satisfied?

You came and I had to fall.
But why did you come at all?

Bulleh, do what you're told:
turn your body to a stove
for the forging of love.
A red-hot rod now hold.

You came and I had to fall.
But why did you come at all?

جس گھر تیرا پھیرا ہویا
سو جبل بل کوئلہ ڈھیر ہویا
جد راکھ اُڈی تد سیر ہویا
کہو کِس گل دا سدھرایا اے
کیوں عِشق اَساں تے آیا اے
توں آیا تے مَیں پایا اے

بُلھا شوہ دے کارن کر!
تن بھٹھی، مَن آہرن کر!
وِچ پریم ہتھوڑا مارن کر!
لوہا بھنجیا، کیس اَٹکایا اے
کیوں عِشق اَساں تے آیا اے
توں آیا تے مَیں پایا اے

Honesty

Hats off to those who a lost coin reimburse,
but have no such scruple about a fat purse.

وارے جا ایٔے اوہناں توں

وارے جا ایٔے اوہناں توں جیہڑے مارن گپ شَڑَپ
گوڈی لَبّھی دے دیوَن، تے بَغچہ گھاؤ گھپ!

I'm not Talking of Here

I told the spirits to go
and I would quickly follow,
but I threw up a screen, so
I would not stand out clear.

> I'm not talking of here,
> that's why I quake with fear.

This world has bound me fast;
even if I'm first, I'm last.
What use are these assets, alas,
my balance sheet is up there.

> I'm not talking of here,
> that's why I quake with fear.

مَیں گل اوتھے دِی کردا ہاں!

نال رُوحاں دے لارا لایا

تُسی چپلو! مَیں نالے آیا

اِتھے پردہ حَیا بنایا

مَیں بھرم بھلایا پھردا ہاں

مَیں گل اوتھے دی کر دا ہاں

پُر گل کردا بھی ڈر دا ہاں

نال عالم دے کھیڈ اَساڈی

جے مَیں میری تاں وِی پھاڑی

دھری دھرائی پُونجی ہاڈی

مَیں اگلا لیکھا بھردا ہاں

مَیں گل اوتھے دی کر دا ہاں

پُر گل کردا بھی ڈر دا ہاں

When robbed I shook with grief
and ran hard after the thief,
and found a clue. Now I've
made plundering my career.

   I'm not talking of here,
   that's why I quake with fear.

دے پُونجی مُورکھ جھنجھلایا

چوراں پِچھّے پَیرا لایا

چوراں دِی مَیں پَیر لِیایا

ہر شب دھاڑے دھڑدا ہاں

مَیں گل اوتھے دی کر دا ہاں

پَر گل کردا بھی ڈر دا ہاں

Desertion

He has left me to my fears.

What was my sin?

Sleep is a stranger now.
I'm streaked with tears.

What was my sin?

Arrows of love are keener
than knives and spears.

What was my sin?

For sheer cruelty, love
has no peers.

What was my sin?

مَینوں چھڈ گئے

مَینوں چھڈ گئے، آپ لد گئے
مَیں وِچ کیہہ تقصیر
راتیں نیندر نہ سُکھ سُتّی
دِنے پلٹیا نِیر
مَیں وِچ کیہہ تقصیر

چھویاں تے تلواراں کولوں
تِکّھے عشق دے تیر
مَیں وِچ کیہہ تقصیر

عشقے جیڈ نہ ظالم کوئی
ایہہ زحمت بے پیر
مَیں وِچ کیہہ تقصیر؟

Relatively Speaking

A stove is better than Bulleh,
it cooks something at least.

When beggars get together
of morsels they make a feast.

Love is a pinprick, Bulleh,
to a slaughterhouse beast.

بُلھے نالوں چُلھا چنگا

بُلھے نالوں چُلھا چنگا
جِس پر تام پکائی دا

رَل فقیراں محبلس کیتی
بھورا بھورا کھائی دا

بُلّھا شوہ نوں سوئی پاوے
جیہڑا اکبرا بنے قصائی دا

Because of You

Because of you, my love,

because of you

my heart trembles like a shadow on water

because of you

if you speak, no one can stop my chatter

because of you

when you sleep I sleep, when you walk I
follow

because of you

till love has besieged you life is hollow,

because of you, my love,

because of you.

توں نہیّوں مَیں ناہیں

توں نہیّوں مَیں ناہیں وے سَجناں
توں نہیّوں مَیں ناہیں
کھولے دے پرچھانویں وانگوں گھوم رہیا مَن ماہیں
توں نہیّوں مَیں ناہیں
جاں توں بُلانویں نالے بولاں چُپ کراں مَیں ناہیں
توں نہیّوں مَیں ناہیں
جاں سواں تاں نالے سونویں جاں ٹراں توں راہیں
توں نہیّوں مَیں ناہیں
بُلّھا شوہ گھر آیا ساڈے جِند ڑی گھول گھمائیں
توں نہیّوں مَیں ناہیں وے سَجناں
توں نہیّوں مَیں ناہیں

Plea for Protection

Take me, love, under your care;
my woes are too much to bear.

> This troubled heart lacks grace
> and laughs in my face.
> When I ask a question
> it takes like a hawk to the air.

> > Take me, love, under your care;
> > my woes are too much to bear.

Love is a raging river
in whose tumult I quiver
and which sucks me under,
while dark clouds shake their hair.

> > Take me love, under your care:
> > my woes are too much to bear.

In the basket you tote
pains writhe. A coiled rope
gleams like a snake.
None can escape your snare.

> > Take me, love, under your care;
> > my woes are too much to bear.

تُسی کرو اَساڈی کاری

تُسی   کرو   اَساڈی   کاری
نی   کوئی   ہو   گئی   ویدن   بَھاری
ایہہ   دِل   میرے   وچ   وَسدا
بہہ   نال   اَساڈے   ہَسدا
چھچھتی   آں   باتاں   تاں   اُٹھ   نَسدا
لے   کے   بازاں   وَانگ   اُڈاری
تُسی   کرو   اَساڈی   کاری

ہُن   میَں   شَوہ   دَریا   واں   پایاں
بَھاٹھاں   لہراں   دے   مُونہہ   آیاں
گھمن   گھیراں   پکڑ   بھوایاں
اوپروں   برکھا   رین   اندھاری
تُسی   کرو   اَساڈی   کاری

وے   تَیں   کیسے   چنچر   چپائے
تارے   کھاری   بیٹھ   لُکائے
مونجھ   دِی   رسّی   ناگ   بنائے
تیرے   سہراں   توں   بلہاری
تُسی   کرو   اَساڈی   کاری

Saturday

Saturday. How fair your true love is!
You will not get another chance to kiss.
    Saturday, a day
    of coils. Distracted, I roam
    through village and waste
    in harsh light and gloom,

             and am paid with scorn.

    Time hangs on my hands,
    and every discord
    in my path stands.
    My love, each thought

             of you is a thorn.

چھنچھر وار

چھنچھر وار، اتاولے دیکھ سجّن دی سوہ
اَساں مُڑ گھر پھیر نہ آ‎ونا جو ہوئی ہو سو ہو

واہ چھنچھر وار وہیلے
دُکھ سجّن دے مَیں وَل پیلے
ڈھونڈاں اوجڑ، جنگل، بیلے
اَدھّری رین، کولڑے وِیلے
بِرہوں گھیریاں

گھڑی پلک تاڈیں تانگھاں
راتیں، سُتڑے شیرا او لانگھاں
اُچّی چڑھ کے کوکاں، چانگھاں
سِینے اندر رڑکن سانگھاں
پیارے تیریاں

Thursday

This is a Thursday. Pain is no sin.
Wearing my dress, love has wandered in.
    A good day to be up
    with wine enough to drown in,
    as I stagger with a cup
    all else forgotten.

        O I'm in ecstasy!

    Think of the simpletons
    who go to be exorcised
    by devilish priests of demons,
    when all they need is a guide

        to set them free

جُمعرات

جُمعرات سُہاونی دُکھ درد نہ آہا پاپ
اوہ جامہ سادا پہن کے آئے تماشے آپ

اگّوں آ گئی جمعرات
شرابوں گا گر مِلی برات
لگّا، مَست، پیالہ ہات
مَینوں بھُلّی ذات صفات
دیوانی ہو رہی

ایسی زَحمت لوک نہ پاون
مُلّاں گھول تعویذ پِلاون
پڑھن عزیمت، جِنّ بُلاون
سّیاں شاہ مدار کھڈاون
مَیں چُپ ہو رہی

Spring

In Spring the fields bloom; every branch is laden
with leaves and flowers like a garlanded woman.

> The girls are rapt in Holi
> while I weep solely
> who succumbed to the folly
> of an unrequited passion.

Holi! Holi!

> Nothing from that to this
> has changed. What was, is.
> That something is amiss
> love should be told. Mention

you miss him sorely.

پھاگن

پھاگن پھولے کھیت حبیبوں بَن تَن پھُول سِنگار
ہر ڈالی پھُل پتّیاں؛ گل پھُولن کے ہار

ہوری کھیلن سِیّاں پھگّن
میرے نین جھلاریں وَگن
اوکھے جِیون دے دن تگّن
سِینے بان پریم دے لگّن
ہوری ہورہی

جو کُجھ روز ازل تھیِں ہوئی
لکھی قلم نے میڈے کوئی
دُکھاں سولاں دِتی ڈھوئی
بُلّھا! شوہ نوں اَکھو کوئی
جس نوں رورہی

Rain

Rain on time brings joy to all
is what the koels call.

Sweet sounds the flute,
boys and girls are at play.
now my sighs bear fruit,
love has come to stay.

Barriers fall.

Friends hurry to my side
with 'Lucky, lucky you.'
My mentor, my guide
made my dreams come true.

Love is all.

ساوَن

ساوَن سو ہے مینگھلا، گھٹ سو ہے کرتار
''ٹھور ٹھور عِنایت وَسّے'' پیہا کرے پُکار

سوہݨ ملہاراں سارے ساوَن
دوتی دُکھ لگے اُٹھ جاوَن
ِنینگر کھِیڈن، کُڑیاں گاوَن
مَیں گھر رنگ رنگیلے ۔ آوَن
آساں پُنیاں

میریاں آساں رَبّ پُچائیاں
سیّاں دین مُبارک آئیاں
مَیں تاں اُن سنگ اکھیاں لائیاں
شاہ عنایت رنگ لگائیاں
آساں پُنیاں

Knots

How many knots shall I tie,
     dear, tell me true?
Forty days to the wedding,
     so forty will do.
Father has told me I must
     go to the bourne
of my in-laws, from which
     none shall return.
The first knot I opened, and
     grumbled and cried,
should the dresses be sequinned,
     or should they be dyed?
I went off to the market with
     an empty purse,
and the merchants supplied me
     a push and a curse.

At last when the fortieth
     knot was undone,
those who had finished their chores
     was nary a one.
The loud procession is here,
     this is the day
when the ready and the unready will
     be taken away.
to be with the master and
     sit by his side
remembering nothing at all but
     she's his bride.
Now the last rites are ended, and
     the bright room
is empty of guests. No one there
     but bride and groom.

گنڈھاں

کہوُ سرتی گلّ کاج دی مَیں گنڈھاں کیتیاں پاواں
سا ہے تے جنج آوسی ہُن جپاھلی گنڈھ گھتاواں
بابل آکھیا آن کے تیں ساہوریاں گھر جانا
ریت اوتھوں دی اور ہے مُڑ پیر نہ ایتھے پانا
گنڈھ پہلی نوں کھول کے مَیں بیٹھی برلاواں
اوڑک جاون جاونِاں، ہُن مَیں ڈاج رنگاواں
دیکھوں طرف بزار دی، سب رستے لاگے
پلّے کجھ نہ روکڑی سب مُجھ سے بھاگے

کر بسم اللہ کھولیاں مَیں گنڈھاں چپاھلی
جس اپنا آپ وِنجھالیا سو سُرجن والی
جنج سوہنی مَیں بھاوندی، لگھیندا آوے
جس نوں عشق ہے لال دا سو لال ہو جاوے
عقل فکر سب چھوڑ کے شہ نال سدھائے
کنتوں بن، گلّ غیر دی اَساں یاد نہ کائے
ہُن انا لِلّٰہ آکھ کے تم کرو نِگاہیں
اللہ ہی سب ہو گیا، عبداللہ ناہیں

GLOSSARY

اتاولے	Swift; speedy
اُت	That
اچنبھا	Wander; strange and new matter
اڈمبر	Apparatus; things
اساتھوں	From us
اشنائی	Friendship
اصلا	In the least
اِکسے	Alike
الانبھا	Complaint
اوّلڑا	Outrageous; crazy
اوگنہاری	Sinful; worthless
اوڑک	At last
آواگون	Transmigration of souls
اوجڑ	There is no way
ابھماں	Pride; haughtiness
بان	Arrow
باندی	Maid servant
باجھ	Without; except
بحر	Ocean
بردا	Slave
بگھصیلا	Wolf

بوہٹن	To arrive
بید	Sacred book; Ved
بھاہ	Fire
بھٹھ	Furnace
بھرواسا	Hope
بھروٹا	Basket
بھگوا	Brownish
بھلیرے	Good
بھورا بھورا	Small pieces; crumbs
بھیت	Secret; mystery
پاندھی	Traveller
پاندھا	Astrologer
پاسا	Pure gold
پسارن	To extend
پنتھ	A Path, sect
پُنیاں	Full moon
پوتھی	Books
پُور	Hatch; a boat load
پون	Wind
پیٹھ	Texture of cloth
پنیسی	Cloth having five hundred threads in the width
پھاون	To entangle
پھاتے	Trapped
تام	Food

تارن ہارا	Protector
تت	Essence
تجن	To abandon; to leave
تس	He; she; it; that
تگن	To sew up
تکڑی	Necklace of three strings
تیاگ	Leaving; abandoning
تیرتھ	Holy place of Hindus
ٹوکاں	Hindrances
ٹھاکردوارا	Idol temple
ٹھانا	Place
ٹھور	Place
جالن	To endure
جت وچ	Wherever
جچدا	To be pleasant and agreeable
جرے	A hunting bird
جیوڑا	Heart
جھالن	To suffer
جھب	Quickly
جھلار	Wheel fixed on the bank of a river, canal, or pond for irrigation purposes
جھنڈولی	One whose hair is of a medium length
جھیڑدے	To quarrel with
چاوڑ	Destruction

چاویں	For the sake of pleasure
چاون	To lift
چتارن	To remind
چوسی	Having four hundred threads in the width of a cloth
چولڑی	Necklace with four strings
چوپڑ	Grease
چُونی	Dust and fragments of precious stones
چھتر	Large umbrella
چھجلی	Winnowing instrument
چھنج	Wrestling
خاسا	A kind of fine muslin
خوار	Distressed; wandering about
خوید	A kind of precious cloth
داج	Dowry
ڈبڑی	Lean
دُرمعانی	Essence of truth (literally 'pearl of meaning')
دُلڑی	Necklace with two strings
دُوتی	Enemy
دیوال	Wall
دھاڑا	Plunder
دُھراں توں	From the very beginning
دھرمسال	Religious place
دھڑوائی	Plunderer

دھوتر	Very thin coarse kind of cotton cloth
ڈھانڈ	Fire
ڈھکن	To arrive
ڈھلکن	To slip down
ڈھوئی	Approach
راج گہیلوی	Companion
رتّا	Dyed; red
رخت	Luggage
رضا	Will; pleasure
رمز	Hint
روکڑی	Money
رین	Night
رجھاون	To please
رکھ	Ashes; forest
زار و زاری رونا	To weep bitterly
سانگ	Spear; mimicry
ساہے	The time fixed by the astrologer
سحرے	Magicians
سُفنے	Dreams
شگھڑا	Obedient
سنیوہڑا	Message
سنگ	Besides
سُہاون	Pleasing
سوہن	Pleasing

سوہدن	To correct
سوگندی	Fragrant
سودھرمی	A good believer
سیس	Head
شوہ	Lover
کامن	The jugglery performed by women at the time of marriage
کام	Desire; love; lust
کبڑی	Hump-backed
کت	Which
کچی	Foolish
کرن	To be poured or cast
کرودھ	Rage
کرڑا	Hard
کلال	Distiller; Seller of spirits
کسنبا	Safflower, a plant yielding red dye
کنت	Husband
گوڑ	Ignorant
گوڑ پسارا	False world
کوچی	Ugly
کوڑے	Ignorant
کھاری	Small basket
کھوہ	Dilapidated building
گدوں	An ass

گڈن	To be set
گردے	Around
گُسائیں	Saint
گنڈھ پاون	To appoint a day for the wedding
گوُنوُگوُنی	Different
لج	Honour; well rope
لگڑ	A kind of hawk used in hunting
لوچ	To desire
مارگ	Way
ماندے	Tired
متیں	Advices
مقدم	Revenue officer
مُول	Principal of a debt; at all; completely
مدھ ماتے	Intoxicated
ناد	Sound
نحو	Grammar
ندان	Ignorant by reason of extreme youth
نڈھا	Young boy
نڑا	Shuttle
نینگر	Boy
نینگر	Girl
واسی	Inhabitant
وت	Again
ودھی	Manner; way

وِسارݨ	To forget
ول ول	Again and again
دلاوݨ	To amuse
ونج	Business
ونجایا	To waste time
وہاجݨ	To purchase
وید	Holy book of Hindus
ویدݨ	Illness
ویرا	Time
وڈھ پرواریا	Man with a large family
ہاویہ	Depths of Hell
ہٹکݨ	To stop
ہنکار	Egotism
ہوری	Hindu festival
ہوکا	Proclamation
ہنسیاری	Ruthless
ہیݨی	Worthless

INDEX OF FIRST LINES

Accursed   78

Acquaintance   90

A for Allah   40

All Cotton-bolls are White   108

A Safe Place   52

A Topsy-turvy World   66

Because of You   200

Be Silent Now   88

Briefing Bulleh   74

Clay   150

Come See Me Once in a While   130

Desertion   196

Does Anyone Know?   70

Dogs are Better than You   126

Embrace Me, Love   54

استھائیاں دی فہرست

پتّیاں لِکھاں مَیں شام نُوں 79

بھرواسا کیہہ اشنائی دا 91

(ا۔ اللہ دِل رتّا میرا 41

سَب اِکو رنگ کپاہیں دا 109

چل بُتّھا! چل اوتھے چلیے 53

اُلٹے ہور زمانے آئے 67

تُوں نہیوں مَیں ناہیں 201

چُپ کرکے کریں گزارا 89

یَگّھے نُوں سمجھاون آئیاں 75

مَائی قدم کریندی یار 151

کدِی آمِل یار پیاریا!... 131

مَینوں چھڈ گئے 197

بُتّھا! کیہہ جاناں مَیں کون 71

گئے تیتھوں اُتّے 127

اپنے سنگ رَلائیں 55

Enough of Learning, Friend   116

From the First Moment   170

Gather Round Me, Friends   156

God has Come Down as Man   162

Heritage   60

Honesty   190

I'm Not Talking of Here   192

I'm Waiting   164

I'm Harbouring a Thief   154

I Swallowed the Hook   46

I'm in a Trap   84

I'm just a Sweepress   166

Knots   212

Left Alone   56

Lass, Look to Your Spinning   132

Love Comes on Bright New Wings   112

Love's Arrival   186

عِلموں بس کریں او یار 117

مَینوں لگڑا عشق 171

مِل لے سہیلڑیو 157

مَولا آدمی بَن آیا 163

اَمّاں بابے دِی بھلیائی! 61

وارے جائیے اوہناں توں 191

مَیں گل اوتھے دی کردا ہاں! 193

مَیں اُڈیکاں کر رہی 165

میری بُکّل دے وچ چور! 155

آپے پاُئیاں کُنڈیاں 47

جندکڑی کے دے منہ آئی 85

مَیں چُوہڑھ ھیڑی آں 167

گنڈھاں 213

اُٹھ چلے گوّانڈھوں یار 57

کرکٹن وَل دھیان کُٹرے 133

عِشق دِی نویوں نویں بہار 113

کیوں عِشق اَساں تے آیا اے 187

My Love has Come to Call   144

Names   128

Neither Hindu, nor Muslim   176
Not for a Moment   68

Obfuscation   178
One is Enough   62

Penitence   140
Plea for Protection   202

Relatively Speaking   198
Rituals   106
Rain   210

Spell   58
Spring   208
Saturday   204
Stop the Spining-wheel, Girl   122
Strange are the Ways of My Love   172

گھڑیالی دیو نکال نی 145

گل سمجھ لئی تے رولا کیہ 129

ہندو نہیں، نہ مُسلمان 177

ایک حرف سی حرفی 69

ہو رنیں سبھے گلڑیاں 179

اِک نقطے وچ گل مُکدی اے 63

کیسی توبہ 141

ٹسی کرو اساڈی کاری 203

بکھے نالوں چُلھا چنگا 199

روزے حج نماز نی مائے 107

ساون 211

اِک ٹوٹا 59

پُھاگن 209

چھنڑ چھر وار 205

گت گڈوے، نہ وَت گڈوے 123

واہ واہ رمز سُجن دی 173

The Benighted 152

The Broken Spinning-wheel 100

The Buyer 110

The Difference 42

The Follower 80

The Load 168

The Lover's Way 104

The Semi-literate 180

The Story of Creation 182

The Transformation 102

The Trap 48

The World is a Fun-fair 96

This Mad Lover 138

Truth Will out 158

Thursday 206

Up With Your Veil, Love 148

Wanderer, Ho 76

Wayfarer, Arise 44

مُلاں تے مشاٹچی... 153

ڈھلک گئی چرخے دی ہتھی......................... 101

سے ونجارے آئے... 111

جیسی صُورت ع دی... 43

تیرے عشق نچائیاں... 81

مَیں گسئنْبا چُن چُن ہاری......................... 169

دھر مسال دھڑوائی وسدے......................... 105

پا پڑھیاں توں نسداہاں میں......................... 181

ہُن مَیں لکھیا سوہنایار......................... 183

"رانجھا رانجھا" کر دی......................... 103

آئی رُت شگوفیاں والی......................... 49

خَلق تماشے آئی یار......................... 97

کوئی پُچھو دِلبر کیہ کر دا......................... 139

جُمعرات... 207

مُنہ آئی بات نہ رہندی اے......................... 159

گھونگھٹ اوہلے نہ لُک سجنا!......................... 149

پا نڈھیا ہو!... 77

اَب تو جاگ !... 45

Whatever You Touch	86
Where is Your Home?	50
Who Choose Cold-hearted Dears	142
Who's Keeping the Gossips Busy?	92
With Love my Heart Overflows	98

جو رنگ رنگیا گوہڑا رنگیا 87

اپݨا دَس ٹِکاٹھا 51

رِکیہ بیدَرداں دے سنگ یاری! 143

چلو دیکھیے اوس مستانڑے نُوں 93

دل لوچے مَاہی یار نُوں 99